THE VALOUR AND THE HORROR

From the Film Series by Brian McKenna and Terence McKenna

THE VALOUR AND THE HORROR

THE UNTOLD STORY OF CANADIANS IN THE SECOND WORLD WAR

By

Merrily Weisbord and Merilyn Simonds Mohr

HarperCollins*Publishers*Ltd

Based on the television series "The Valour and the Horror" directed by Brian
McKenna and produced in collaboration with the Canadian Broadcasting
Corporation, the National Film Board of Canada, Société Radio-Canada and
Telefilm Canada

Cover painting: Detail of *Normandy Countryside* by Bruno Borak courtesy Canadian
War Museum, Ottawa; Photo: for Canadian War Museum by William Kent

First Edition

Design: Peter Maher
Production: Paula Chabanais & Associates

Canadian Cataloguing in Publication Data

Weisbord, Merrily
The Valour and the horror

"From the film series by Brian McKenna and Terence McKenna"
ISBN 0-00-215744-6

1. World War, 1939-1945 — Canada. 2. World War, 1939-1945 — Personal
narratives, Canadian.
I. Mohr, Merilyn. II. Title. III. Title: Valour and the horror (Television program).

D768.15.W45 1991   940.53'71   C91-095262-0

 91 92 93 94 95 AG 5 4 3 2 1

Acknowledgements

The authors thank the veterans and their families for sharing their stories, without which this book would not have been possible.

We gratefully acknowledge the research of the many people who worked on the film series *The Valour and the Horror*, particularly Roman Jarymowycz, D'Arcy O'Connor and Susan Purcell.

Of special interest were the war memoirs of Canadian soldiers William Allister, *Where Life and Death Hold Hands* (Stoddart, 1989); J.Douglas Harvey, *Boys, Bombs and Brussels Sprouts* (McClelland and Stewart, 1981); and Donald Pearce, *Journal of a War* (Macmillan of Canada, 1965).

Our appreciation to Louise Abbott, Ann Diamond and Mary-Ellen Gariepy for their typing assistance; to Mark Achbar for help in a crisis; to historian Victor Suthren of the Canadian War Museum for vetting the manuscript; to Anna Paskal for photo research; to Iris Skeoch for organizing the production of this book; to Assistant Editor Laura Krakowec; and to Rebecca Vogan for copy-editing.

Our *croix de guerre* go to Arnie Gelbart and Wayne Grady.

We dedicate this book to all our sons and daughters.

War is not like you think, running up a hill, firing away. It's more like the two of us sitting here and some son-of-a-bitch eight miles away says: "Hey, let's kill somebody over there." And they fire a shell and it blows us to pieces.

WALTER JENKINS,
a survivor of the Battle of Hong Kong

Table of Contents

The Valour and the Horror

Prologue

On a grey November morning in 1987, Brian McKenna stood with his 11-year-old daughter, Robin, in front of the Westmount Cenotaph, in Montreal, Quebec. It was Remembrance Day, and McKenna and his daughter were watching the old soldiers with their berets and clinking medals, remnants of another era.

Suddenly Robin pointed to the inscriptions carved on the base of the war memorial.

"Dad, here's Adrian Harold McKenna. Who is he?"

"Robin, I know he was a relative," he replied, "but I don't know anything else about him. I don't know his story."

His daughter's question triggered in McKenna an obsession to tell the stories of Canadians at war. Not a military account of campaigns, but the true stories of the men who suffered the day-to-day reality of battle. His search for Adrian led McKenna and his brother, Terence, to produce *The Killing Ground*, a two-hour documentary film on the First World War. They then continued, without interruption, to the Second World War, producing the six-hour film series — *The Valour and the Horror* — on which this book is based.

"The guys who went through the two world wars," says Brian McKenna, "the young men who died and those who came back, many mutilated in mind and body, are owed at least this much: that their stories be told properly and in context."

It was as if McKenna had been training all his life for the task. One of his first assignments as a young journalist was covering the 25th anniversary of D-Day in 1969. Five years later he returned to Normandy, not to the graveyards and memorials, but to the landing beaches and the villages, where he walked with veterans and listened to their stories. As a founding producer of CBC's *The Fifth Estate*, the Canadian Broadcasting Corporation's investigative documentary series, he directed some 60 films, often reporting from the world's military hotspots.

In the course of his work, McKenna confronted war first-hand — the aftermath of the Khmer Rouge war in Cambodia, the so-called "low-intensity wars" in El Salvador and Nicaragua, torture in Argentina, war criminals in Canada. In his investigation of war, he discovered how war is usually reported — "lied about, distorted, used as propaganda and ultimately repressed." McKenna's goal in his films about the First and Second World Wars was to unearth "the small essential stories that were never told properly, or that leaked out incompletely after the wars."

In *The Valour and the Horror*, Brian McKenna chose to concentrate on three major struggles: the Battle of Hong Kong, in which almost 2,000 recruits, many untrained, were quickly overwhelmed in a desperate battle, then imprisoned in Japanese "slave" labour camps for over four years; Bomber Command, in which 10,000 air crew died in a secret campaign that massacred at least half a million German civilians; and Normandy, where soldiers suffered the devastating casualties of trench warfare despite ingenious military strategies.

The facts of these campaigns were not hard to find. But the cold calculation of men lost and machines "killed" did not reflect the reality of life on the battlefield. As McKenna discovered when he began to trace Adrian, the individual stories of enlisted men are rarely part of official history.

From the Cenotaph that November day, McKenna went to Westmount Library, where he asked for a record of those named on the memorial. There was none. The research librarian suggested City Hall, but no records were found there either. "They didn't know who the men were. Their stories were lost." It was in Ottawa, at the National Personnel Records Office, that McKenna finally found the original file of Adrian Harold McKenna. And a series of uncanny connections.

"He was my grandfather's younger brother. He graduated from Montreal's Loyola College, as I did, at age 21. And when

I found his medical record, it sent chills down my spine. When I'm under stress — filming war in San Salvador or Beirut — the first thing that goes is my stomach. It turns to fire. And when 22-year-old Adrian Harold McKenna was unloaded at the Front outside Ypres in 1915, the first thing that went was his stomach. 'Infirm stomach,' reads the report. All through the terrible winter of 1915: 'Infirm stomach.' Back to the Front: 'Infirm stomach.' "

The last entry in Adrian's medical record reads, "Killed in action, bullet through the right lung, January 16, 1916." A paragraph in his Regimental history records that he was shot at night, in no-man's land. By the time the stretcher-bearers went to get him in the morning, he had bled to death.

The enlistment papers led McKenna to old family photographs, where they found a picture of 12,000 men lined up in the park on Fletcher's Field, at the base of Mount Royal.

"There's a little guy standing in the middle with a balloon hand-drawn over his head, saying, 'It's me.' And it was Adrian, standing right in front of the house where I used to live on Esplanade."

This was the voice from the past that made Brian McKenna determined to learn all he could about the Canadian experience of war.

"The suffering that I felt while learning about my grandfather's brother made me finally understand things about my family — the silences that I've never understood before, the gaps in our collective memory.

"There's no family in this country that has not been touched by war. The pain goes very deep. When they returned from the Front, the men who were soldiers kept their stories inside, not telling them, but still suffering and afflicting others with their suffering."

The Valour and the Horror is based on interviews with hundreds of soldiers. Some tell their stories directly on film. Others are represented by actors who recreate the immediacy of the mens' experience. One chose to use a pseudonym, the horrors of the battlefield still too fresh to confront.

Three hundred people — researchers, interviewers, writers, producers, directors, actors and technicians — worked on the film series. With the full support of the Chief of the Defence Staff, it was shot at Canadian military bases in Farnham,

Brian McKenna

Quebec; in Camp Gagetown, New Brunswick; at the Second World War air-force training base in Hamilton, Ontario. McKenna incorporated evocative paintings from the cache of war art buried in a streetcar barn in Ottawa. He took Hong Kong veterans back to Japanese POW camps in Kawasaki and Niigata; documented Bomber Command pilots meeting women who had survived the firebombing of Hamburg; and, with the Canadian commanders, he visited the Norman ridge where Canadians suffered the highest losses since Dieppe. The film research provided the material for this book.

"The Canadian instinct is not to speak or write about war," says McKenna, "the belief being that if you do not give the horror a name, perhaps it will never return. But the truth we don't face is that in the Normandy campaign, for example, we had more dead per capita than Britain or the United States. In the Second World War, more than a million men and women were in uniform — 41 percent of the male population aged 18 to 45 — and 42,000 died. In the First World War, we sent 600,000 Canadians overseas, 100,000 more than the Americans had in Operation Desert Storm. We were 9 million people and the 60,661 Canadians who died represented the highest death toll per capita of any Allied nation. All this from a country that considers itself unwarlike."

As McKenna discovered at the Cenotaph, the consequence of silence is ignorance.

"By failing to speak about war, we deny our children part of their birthright. We do not celebrate valour and we do not expose the horror."

Prompted by his daughter, inspired by the haunting voice of his great-uncle, *The Valour and the Horror* offers a dramatic, fresh insight into the lives of the Canadians who fought in the Second World War.

Prisoners of War: Surviving Hong Kong

CHAPTER ONE

Tied to a lamp-post at the Star Ferry Wharf in Kowloon, Private John Gray watched as an officer of the Imperial Japanese Army raised his sword. Flames lit the sky. The air was filled with smoke from a burning oil refinery. As one, the squad of soldiers shouldered their rifles and took aim.

Their target was a farm boy from Langruth, Manitoba. Canada had been at war for over two years, Gray in the Canadian army for just seven months, in Hong Kong, only three weeks. Most of his buddies had escaped to the island, commandeering every available boat. A few had taken advantage of the confusion, broken ranks with their Regiments and were roving the streets of Kowloon looking for pretty Chinese girls in low-cut red silk dresses, offering a "long time" for a single Hong Kong dollar. Even as the Japanese army rolled southward into the city, some soldiers were having the time of their lives. Whether Gray was among the carousers or simply struggling to retreat through the chaos will never be known. Somewhere, two Chinese civilians jumped him, dragged him out to the street and turned him over to a Japanese infantry patrol. He was interrogated in flawless English by the Kempeti, a Japanese version of the Gestapo.

Private John Gray, 21, from Langruth, Manitoba, was the first Canadian infantryman to die in combat in the Second World War.

Six Japanese soldiers cocked their rifles. The sun glinted on the upraised sword. The Kempeti officer nodded. The sword fell, and a volley of bullets tore into the eighth child of Robert and Isabel Gray. It was December 13, 1941. On that day, John Gray became a footnote to history: the first Canadian infantryman to die in combat in the Second World War.

Gray was a rifleman with The Winnipeg Grenadiers, one of two underequipped and poorly trained Canadian battalions that had arrived in the British colony for what had been billed

John Payne, 21, from Winnipeg,
Manitoba, with his mother
Margaret, sisters Yvonne (left) and
Dianne and brother Ben, leaving
home for Hong Kong.

as simple garrison duty. With Canada's top units guarding
Britain, the only men left for the Hong Kong mission were
these recruits — officially designated as "not recommended for
operational consideration." They were told their only
responsibility would be maintaining a garrison, a visible
presence, in the face of the Japanese, who were at war in
neighbouring China. Even if the Japanese attacked, said the
British general commanding Hong Kong, the enemy was only
5,000 strong. Japanese troops were ill-equipped and
unaccustomed to night fighting; they had little artillery
support; their aircraft were mostly obsolete and their pilots
"mediocre, unable to do dive-bombing because of poor
eyesight."

In fact, the Canadians arrived to face the seasoned victors of
the Sino-Japanese war: determined, dedicated and disciplined
soldiers who would within three weeks overwhelm the garrison
and claim the island of Hong Kong for their own.

THE RECRUITS

The 2,000 Canadians who joined the 10,000 Commonwealth
troops already stationed in Hong Kong were hardly more than
boys. Some had signed up to fight for King and country, others
because their fathers had served in the First World War and it was
the manly thing to do. Some joined to fight Fascism. Still others

The Winnipeg Grenadiers, "not recommended for operational consideration," boarding the train for Vancouver en route to Hong Kong, October 25, 1941.

enlisted because their buddies did; it would be a lark.

Private Armand Bourbonnière left Deerhorn, Manitoba, to join The Winnipeg Grenadiers because his mother gave away his skates.

"Well, I went up to Grade Nine. I would have kept on going to school, but my Dad had a heart attack and I had to miss school two weeks a month to drive trucks. I would always go back, but I wasn't interested anymore because I got so far behind the other children I could never catch up. So one day I says to my Dad, 'Well, there's no use, you know. I can't get nowhere.'

"Anyway, I used to like skating a lot, hockey, and I was quite good at it. And my mother gave my skates away. I got mad and joined the service. And I had an older brother. He decided to join because I was in there. We joined the same Regiment."

Bob Manchester, 25 years old, was the 27th young man to enlist in The Winnipeg Grenadiers. "Canada started looking at the possibility of going to war and a group of us, all non-active militia, were called into the armory. We were read the Riot Act and told what the situation was, and asked for volunteers. Well, 90 percent of the guys volunteered." It was the third of September, 1939, the day before Canada declared war on Germany.

"Then as soon as the word went out that the war was on and that Canada had agreed to mobilize the troops, chaos started pouring into Winnipeg from all points west and northeast, and south. They came in as volunteers and started building up the Regiment."

Bob Manchester, 25, Winnipeg, Manitoba, soon after his enlistment in The Winnipeg Grenadiers.

They didn't practice actual battle manoeuvres and when they arrived in Hong Kong, they had only the most rudimentary weapons training.

Bob "Flash" Clayton, 19, from Toronto, Ontario, while serving in Newfoundland, 1941.

"We had done nothing but rifle examination, machine-gun experimentation. Most of the chaps had little or no experience handling weapons such as grenade launchers, rifle grenade launchers, mortar launchers, hand grenades. No mines, land mines or any of the more sophisticated weapons.

"And most of the men had not even thrown dummy grenades. In fact, when we arrived in Hong Kong we were trying to train the young lads how to load a grenade. First of all, the grenade is empty till you put the primer in. You have a box of primers. Well, what you do is you prime maybe two or three dozen for your detonating use. But if they're not primed, they're no damn good. It doesn't react at all. You can pull the pin and throw the thing. It won't fire. It's the pin coming out that sets the primers that sets the explosion. They didn't even get that training. In battle, some of the men were throwing empty grenades."

Bob Clayton, a wiry young man nicknamed Flash, was a sergeant with The Royal Rifles of Canada, the other battalion sent to Hong Kong.

"I went in the militia when I was 14. They didn't care in those days, you know. Kids didn't have any money. It was the Depression. I was one of eight kids and my Dad didn't have a job. So us kids, we went down and joined the army. And we loved it. A week before the war started, I get a call to report to the army. I didn't know what was going on. They said to come in my uniform. So I went in my uniform. My Ma said, "Where you going?" And I just tore out the door and never said nothing, down to the armory. And the next thing we were issued rifles, were in trucks and on our way to do guard duty on the Welland Canal. And while we were there, Canada officially went to war.

"In 1940, I was with The Royal Rifles of Canada, in Sussex, New Brunswick, for a while and then we went over to Newfoundland where we did guard duty. The first was up at Gander, then at Botwood, then St. John's. I wasn't in St. John's long because they sent me on a six-week infantry course on all weapons. Start out with a .22 and go up to two-inch mortars, then Boys anti-tank rifle, Thompson submachine gun. You went through every weapon used in the army. Soon as I went to the Regiment, they made me a sergeant. And I got to be Sergeant of 14th platoon."

Clayton's level of training was unusual. As he says, "Most of our fellows were on guard duty all the time, so they didn't get the chance to get the training they should have done."

Fred Reich, a 22-year-old private in The Grenadiers, A Company, remembers that, "Prior to leaving to go to Hong Kong we must have got about 700 reinforcements. A lot of these reinforcements, it might not be nice to say, but they were the rejects from every Regiment from Halifax going west. A lot of these fellows, they certainly should never have been allowed to enlist in the service. A lot of them were unfit, that's all there was to it.

Fred Reich, 22, from Deerhorn, Manitoba.

"And when we got to Hong Kong, they put more emphasis on trying to compete with the Brits, that we could right wheel, left wheel, make straighter lines and all this and all that. We were just playing soldier. We didn't know what to do."

Twenty percent of the men called up for garrison duty in Hong Kong had never fired live ammunition from a rifle; 40 percent had never manned a machine gun. The Rifles had a little practice throwing dummy grenades; The Grenadiers had tossed none at all. Few of these soldiers had ever seen a mortar shell.

"We weren't equipped," adds Bob Clayton. "We didn't have a damn thing. I guess they thought there wouldn't be a war with the Japanese. And it wouldn't have mattered even if we were well trained. Okay, we would have killed a few more of them."

In Vancouver, Clayton, Manchester, Bourbonnière and Reich, together with nearly 2,000 other recruits, were crammed onto the *Awatea*, a passenger-freighter built to hold 540 passengers. The soldiers slept in hammocks slung over mess tables. Conditions aboard the ship were so bad that some of the soldiers mutinied. By jumping ship, scurrying down anchor lines and finding other recondite means of escape, almost 50 men managed to desert by the time the *Awatea* weighed anchor.

Mutiny wasn't the only bad omen. Because of administrative bungling in Ottawa, The battalions' 212 trucks, jeeps and Bren-gun carriers sat on flatcars somewhere on a railway siding in Ontario. A week later, the equipment was loaded onto an American freighter, but it never reached the Canadians. It ended up in the Philippines, where it was captured by the Japanese.

THE BATTLEGROUND

The Battle of Hong Kong contained the elements of a classic tragedy: badly trained, inadequately supplied soldiers thrust innocent and ignorant into a garrison about to be attacked by a disciplined, technologically superior army that outnumbered them five to one.

The epitome of that tragedy was 53-year-old Colonel John Lawson, the Director of Military Training for the Canadian Army. Lawson was a veteran of the First World War and a survivor of Passchendaele. If there was anything the military had learned from that catastrophic battle, it was that if you send an untrained man into combat, he's likely to die. It was Lawson's job to ensure that the recruits sent into the Second World War had thorough basic training — how to handle a rifle and how to throw a grenade. The rest of the training would come in the trial-by-fire of battle itself.

Lawson was also responsible for assessing the battle-readiness of each battalion of Canadian soldiers. In his seasoned judgment, there were really nine unfit for combat. Among these were The Royal Rifles of Canada, a Quebec battalion made up largely of farm boys from the Eastern Townships and the Gaspé — some English, most French — whose motto was "Able and Willing." Another was The Winnipeg Grenadiers, mostly Prairie kids whose Regimental badge was an exploding grenade. The only experience these soldiers had was garrison duty for the Empire — The Rifles in the British colony of Newfoundland, The Grenadiers in Jamaica. In Lawson's opinion, these boys were in need of "refresher training."

Britain had already decided not to buttress the garrison in Hong Kong with English troops. In 1940, seeing war with Japan as a distinct possibility, Churchill argued that reinforcing the garrison would fritter away valuable resources needed to confront the Nazi menace on the Continent. The governor of Hong Kong concurred; he wrote to Whitehall in October, 1940, urging the withdrawal of the British garrison "to avoid the slaughter of civilians and the destruction of property that would follow a Japanese attack." However, few influential Hong Kong Brits and even fewer British War Office personnel believed the Japanese would presume to take on the Commonwealth. Edward Grasett, the British commanding officer in Hong Kong, was among those who were sanguine about their colonial position. Still, he believed the garrison

WRC-2426

Brigadier John K. Lawson, Commanding Officer of the Canadian Forces, with Sir Mark Young, Governor of Hong Kong, November 16, 1941.

could use a few symbolic reinforcements. In July, 1941, retired from his command and en route to England, the Major-General stopped off in Ottawa to visit his old friend, Harry Crerar, the Canadian Chief of the General Staff.

History suggests that this old boys' meeting triggered a tacit understanding. Arriving from Canada, Grasett met with Churchill's Chiefs of Staff and argued that Hong Kong be reinforced; Canada might supply the units. On September 19, a request came from the British government. Would Canada consider sending one or two battalions to bolster the garrison in Hong Kong? Crerar enthusiastically recommended that the Canadian Army take on the job. Not just one battalion — why not send two? The Canadian defence staff urged Prime Minister Mackenzie King to do so as quickly as possible. The British request offered an opportunity to wave the flag. Canada was spending $750 million a year on the war, but no blood had yet been spilled in battle. Sending troops overseas to do something other than garrison duty in England offered good publicity for the war effort at little cost. After all, the British had assured them that Hong Kong was nothing more than another tour of island duty. As warm as Jamaica. As safe as Newfoundland.

The Canadian brass knew nothing of Churchill's memo of January 7, 1941, in which he concluded that the tiny Asian outpost was indefensible and should not be reinforced. "If Japan goes to war with us, there is not the slightest chance of holding Hong Kong or relieving it. It is most unwise to increase the loss we shall suffer there," Churchill wrote ten months before the Canadians were shipped out. "Instead of increasing the garrison, it ought to be reduced to a symbolic scale.... Japan will think long before declaring war on the British Empire, and whether there are two or six battalions at Hong Kong will make no difference to her choice. I wish we had fewer troops there."

Despite a substantial Canadian legation in Tokyo, the Canadian military did not ask for an independent military assessment of the situation in Hong Kong. Canadian military intelligence came exclusively from the British, who were selective in what they shared. In retrospect, it is difficult to comprehend that the Canadian government did not know Japan was close to invading Hong Kong.

Although most Japanese generals and politicians favoured an attack on the Soviet Union north of China, the Emperor had his heart set on crushing the Americans and the British who, from a Japanese perspective, had been enslaving and exploiting the Orient from Singapore to Hong Kong. War records show that, after kicking the Commonwealth troops out of Asia, the Japanese planned to annex British Columbia and Alberta; the rest of Canada would be under the thumb of a Japanese governor general.

Meanwhile, the Imperial Japanese Army had been successfully warring its way through China since 1937. By the summer of 1941, five major Chinese cities had fallen, including Canton, just 80 miles north of Hong Kong.

Thousands of battle-honed troops were massed on the border between China and Hong Kong when Mackenzie King decided Canada would reinforce the island garrison and do its duty for the British Empire. The best soldiers were in England. No matter: they would send The Royal Rifles and The Grenadiers. Hong Kong was only garrison duty and they'd learn as they went along. The man chosen to lead them was Colonel John Lawson — the man who had designated them as unfit for combat.

Within weeks of Mackenzie King's decision, a force was mustered under Commanding Officer Brigadier Lawson. Everything was top secret. The soldiers were sealed aboard transcontinental trains, sent to Vancouver, shipped out with no idea where they were going.

"As far as we were concerned," says Bourbonnière, "when we got to Vancouver we *still* figured we were going to Nanaimo. But they put us on this New Zealand ship. So where could you figure you were going then? We decided we were going to New Zealand. It was a New Zealand ship, eh?"

As the *Awatea* set sail, London cabled Ottawa with the information that there were only 3,000 Japanese troops within a 20-mile radius of Hong Kong.

London was wrong. The Japanese numbered 50,000.

"And," adds Bourbonnière, "if they would have said Hong Kong to us? You say to yourself, you never been to Hong Kong, eh? You're young and you say well, I want to see Hong Kong. I'm going to see Chinese women and everything else, and you're happy to go. Sure, you don't think of fighting. You don't think of the war."

THE GOOD LIFE

November 16, 1941. Hong Kong. The Gibraltar of the Orient.

To the Canadians sailing into the harbour that bright, tropical November morning, Hong Kong looked like a photo-spread from *National Geographic*. As the recruits massed on the deck of the *Awatea* for roll call, rib-sailed junks madly jostled for position, waiting for the ship's garbage to be thrown into the bay. A pale mist hovered over the mountains that framed the city; against the lush green backdrop, rooftops curled in the sun. One by one, the sergeants barked out the names of the men enlisted in The Royal Rifles and The Grenadiers. Bourbonnière. Clayton. Friesen. Manchester. MacKay. Stroud ... At ease. The men grabbed their packs, shouldered their rifles and hurried down the gangplank, past the towering, bearded Sikh guarding the pier in all his crimson glory.

Hong Kong is a British colony consisting of a mainland peninsula and an island about eight miles long and four across, not much bigger than Manhattan. It lies at the end of a chain of islands — Japan, Taiwan, Hong Kong — that arcs off the east coast of southeast China.

On the north shore of the island, a mile across the harbour

Canadian soldiers arriving in Hong
Kong, November 16, 1941.

from the city of Kowloon where the *Awatea* docked, is
Victoria, the capital city. On the south side is the garrison
town of Stanley, guarding the waters of the South China Sea.

Hong Kong "dollar bills," the currency of pleasure to Canadian garrison troops.

The island is known for its hilly terrain interrupted by a pass through the middle, the Wong Nei Chong Gap.

Hong Kong was colonized by British traders mainly to traffic opium on the mainland. In the mid-1800s, the British acquired the peninsula of Kowloon and the island from the Chinese, and in 1898 signed a 99-year lease on the New Territories, extending their holdings 15 miles north from the port of Kowloon to the Chinese border. In 1997 that lease expires, but in 1941 the British were firmly entrenched as colonial masters.

Twenty thousand British civilians lived in Hong Kong, primarily civil servants, affluent traders, businessmen and their families. The richest were ensconced on "The Peak," a lush residential area overlooking Victoria, where they lived on luxurious estates serviced by cheap and plentiful labour drawn from the 1.5 million Chinese in the colony.

Of these, about a million were refugees who had poured in over the past two years, fleeing the Japanese. Many were dying of malnutrition and disease. Early each morning, British government trucks crawled through the mainland city of Kowloon, picking up the bodies of those who had died on the streets and sidewalks the night before.

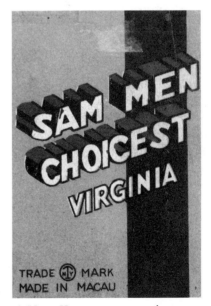

A Hong Kong cigarette package.

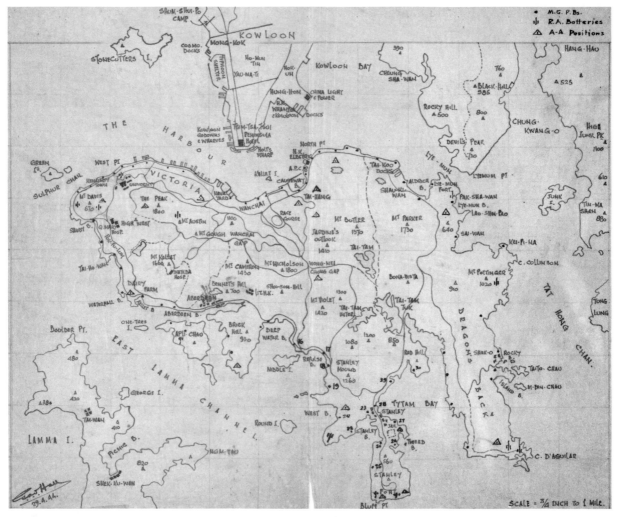

Hong Kong island and its Commonwealth defensive positions, drawn by G.W. Hall during his internment at Sham Shui Po POW camp.

Many of the English in Hong Kong considered the Chinese — even the wealthy, well-educated Chinese — far beneath them. A hundred thousand Chinese lived on junks in the harbour while the Brits swam and boated in Repulse Bay, played polo and attended black-tie affairs at Kowloon's swank Peninsula Hotel. Their lifestyle and colonial isolation made them smug. Even after the arrival of the Canadian soldiers, many British civilians remained convinced that a Japanese invasion was simply out of the question.

As the Canadian recruits marched through the streets of Kowloon, they glimpsed a grotesque mix of poverty and opulence. They saw Mandarins in scarlet robes, Hindus in loincloths. And white men in white suits, faces shadowed by pith helmets, riding high in rickshaws pulled by running, sweating coolies. Beggars anchored every street corner, sores festering, arms and legs eaten away. Flies swarmed over the beggars' stumps and over raw meat hanging in the shop fronts. Under the bright, brassy march of the military band raged a cacophony of hawkers. Shine your shoes for a nickel. Have a girl — some as young as 11 or 12 — for a buck.

The Canadians marched down Nathan Road to the Sham Shui Po Barracks that extended from the harbour towards the mountains of the mainland. In their shiny boots and crisp uniforms, in this startling, fetid place, they thought of the only Oriental images they knew — Marco Polo, Gunga Din, Clark Gable in *China Seas*. At Sham Shui Po Barracks, the Canadians had their first real taste of the good life, colonial style. Ike Friesen, a 21-year-old Russian Mennonite from a Manitoba farm, had hardly seen the bright lights of Winnipeg before he landed in Kowloon.

"We had little batmen in our huts," remembers Friesen. "There were about 40 of us, with three boys in there. They would wake us up in the morning, and they would shave you in bed before you really got your eyes open. And when they finished shaving you, you'd grab your towel and run for the shower. When you got back, your bed would be made and your clothes for the day would be laid out."

For the green young Canadians, the first three weeks in Hong Kong were a hoot. "We were out for a good time," says Friesen. "The pubs were good. The night life was fast. The girls were nice. The night life in Sham Shui Po could show Canada a few tricks that they haven't even seen yet. We had a ball."

Bob Manchester and Bob Clayton remember their introduction to Hong Kong's infamous pleasures — the all-night dance hall philosophically dubbed Gonorrhea Racetrack; the red-light district, Wanchai; the opium dens and Thieves' Row, where anything could be had, for a price. In the words of the soldier's song — cigarettes, whiskey and wild, wild women.

"Everything was cheap," says Manchester. "Beer was ten cents a bottle. Rickshaw rides were ten cents a crack. And you could pick up most anything for a good Canadian buck; long time, short time. Really."

Yielding to impulse, Bob Clayton had a tattoo with "Mother" engraved in the centre.

To these sons of Maritime fishermen and Prairie sod-busters, war and intrigue seemed as exotically unreal as the upturned eaves and dark-haired whores. The real battle, after all, was in Europe.

But they weren't entirely comfortable. They could not

ignore the sick, the crippled and the starving who surged against the barbed wire separating the barracks compound from Kowloon city streets. The soldiers tossed coins to the crowd and watched in horror as the barbed wire ripped into the flesh of the children scrambling for alms.

"What struck me most," recalls Friesen, "and what struck me the hardest, was the first lecture that we got from the British commander. I was a transport driver, and he came out specially to us 'lorry drivers,' as he called us. He said, 'One thing I want to tell you. If you're driving down the streets in the city of Kowloon, if you hit a Chinaman, you look back in your rearview mirror, and if he's still kicking you back that truck up and run over him again. Because if you send him to the hospital, it'll cost you the hospital bill. If you kill him, it'll cost you five dollars for burial.'"

The British army eyed coolies with suspicion. Any one could be a Japanese spy. Orders had been given to shoot spies on sight. A coolie's rags might be fake; his terror contrived. Without interpreters, who could tell if the Chinese "babble" was a denial or a confession? Was he on his way to his controller? Or home to his wife and kids?

"Our kitchen boy was with one of our platoons up in the hills," recalls Friesen, "and the second day they were there, they shot him. They caught him flashing signals across the bay to the Japs. This is what you had to watch for, what we called the fifth columnists. And there was a lot of it. You couldn't trust any of them, but really, you couldn't blame them either." Any promise, any flicker of hope from the Japanese was better to them than what they had.

Racism was rife — and it extended to all Oriental peoples. "All the time people were saying, 'Oh, don't worry about the Japanese,'" says Bob Manchester. " 'They can't bloody well see at night. They're little squirty guys; they don't weigh more than 150 pounds.'" For their part, the Japanese considered Westerners "effeminate and cowardly. They have an intense dislike of fighting in the rain or at night," said one Japanese officer.

To his horror, Manchester would soon experience first-hand the true capacity of the Japanese military. "They had been fighting the goddamn Chinese for years. They'd come all the way down China, massacring from Nanking to Shanghai. There they were sitting at our bloody doorstep and they were raring to go; they wanted some new blood. And they got us. We were just kids."

THE JAPANESE ATTACK

The Japanese High Command chose a Sunday — December 7, 1941 — to order its troops into action across the Pacific.

At 7:50 a.m., in a sneak attack on the American military base at Pearl Harbor, waves of Japanese bombers destroyed the moored Pacific fleet. Within hours, following the sunrise westward, the army of the Emperor attacked the Philippines, Singapore and the British crown colony of Hong Kong. Six hours after Pearl Harbor, 48 Japanese dive bombers destroyed Hong Kong's diminutive air force where it was parked, on the ground.

Within hours, Canada declared war on Japan, the first country to do so, several hours before the United States and a full day before Britain.

Bob Clayton was off-duty, watching a movie at the mainland camp at Sham Shui Po, when the first bombs fell. "It flashed up on the screen, 'All troops return to the barracks.' And back to the barracks we went."

Most of his Regiment left for the island during the initial days of the bombing and he stayed on at the mainland barracks, alone with the new recruits. "The next morning, I had one puttee on, and I was just going to put on the other, when one of the recruits comes running and says, 'Gee Sarge, come out and look at all the airplanes up there.' So I go out and look up and, oh my God Almighty, it wasn't ours. They were very high and in a V. They were high enough that I couldn't make out what the planes were. But once I saw those objects start to drop from the planes, I knew what was going on.

"So, I got a couple of Bren guns and set them up. Told the recruits to spread out around the barracks. We had deep rain ditches there because of the violent storms they get. And I told some of them to get in the ditch beside the gun, and I said, 'As long as those planes stay up that high, don't you be out here on the gun looking at them and trying to hit them, because you're not going to hit them that high. And if they keep bombing you're going to get wounded for nothing. If they start dive-bombing then get out and get on the gun.'

"Well, the Japs just made the one run over. I saw some dead Chinese but none of our fellows were casualties at that time. Then they put us on boats and across the harbour we went."

Shortly after the air raid, the Japanese army attacked. In December, 1941, British Intelligence increased their estimate of the force assembling across from Hong Kong to 5,000 men.

Japanese soldiers parade on the
Chinese mainland after their
successful campaign, 1941.

In fact, ten times that many — at least 50,000 troops — had
been transported by bicycle, horse and truck to the border
between China and the British colony. Superior weapons and
training gave them confidence; the Emperor was their cause.
Hirohito had pledged to bring "peace" to the Far East and
these troops were there to enforce it.

Before leaving Japan, the soldiers had solemnly stood at
Tokyo's Yasakuni Shrine, invoking the spirits of fallen
comrades, warriors who had died in battle and, according to
the ancient Bushido code of the Samurai, had become gods.
Death before surrender. If not death at the hands of the enemy,
then suicide with a knife — *hara kiri*. Surrender was the
ultimate shame; death in combat, the supreme glory.

The commander of the Japanese troops was instructed to
seize Hong Kong in ten days. They had accomplished as much
and more in their push across Manchuria. Poised on the
border, they awaited the signal to attack. *Hana-Saku, Hana-
Saku* was the code: flowers abloom, flowers abloom.

"Through the fence at the border you could see the Japanese stockpiling ammunition and other stuff," recalls Manchester. "Of course the British said, 'Don't worry about them. They're buggering around over there all the time. They're never going to come here.'"

While the Japanese massed on the border, the British rejigged the colony's defences. They had two infantry battalions, British and East Indian, stationed in Hong Kong — about 10,000 men. Also defending the island was the Hong Kong Volunteer Defence Corps — 2,000 British and Chinese civilians armed with First World War weapons. The island was ringed by 72 concrete pillboxes and protected by a series of fixed coastal guns.

The British divided their defences into two brigades: The Mainland Brigade of British and East Indians and The Island Brigade headquartered at Wong Nei Chong Gap, commanded by Lawson, and comprising British, Volunteers and Canadians. The Canadians were sent to the south side of the island — The Grenadiers to the west, The Rifles to the east — ready to repel a beach landing. The commander of the British garrison was certain any invasion would be an amphibious assault from the south, and so the British had placed their guns at that end of the island, facing into the South China Sea.

The sea assault never materialized. Totally unprepared, the Canadians would soon find themselves in a desperate battle against tens of thousands of crack troops flowing into Kowloon and across the narrow strait to the island, to hit them from behind.

By the morning of December 8, Japanese infantry had crossed the Chinese border and marched four miles into British territory. In the early 1930s, the British had built a 12-mile stretch of defensive fortifications designed to block such an invasion. The line was crucial to the defence of Kowloon's huge water reservoir. A chain of tunnels and First World War style trenches honeycombed the mountain, punctuated by concrete bunkers that were christened after the invincible old Empire — Shaftesbury Avenue, Charing Cross. This was the place where John Gray did point duty the day before he was shot — the place where the British believed the garrison troops could repel any hordes foolish enough to attack. Whimsically, the English called it the Gin Drinker's Line because it overlooked Gin Drinker's Bay. The name was reminiscent of smartly dressed, red-faced English officers poised on a tropical terrace, cool drink in steady hand.

To reach this key British fortification, the Japanese had to march 25 miles through the mountains, practically to the lip of the reservoir. The British calculated the journey would take a week. The Japanese did it in a day.

Two days after Pearl Harbor, in the dead of night, using grappling hooks to climb the sheer cliffs, the Japanese reached the concrete bunkers of the Gin Drinker's Line.

"This Japanese officer came along with ten men on a reconnaissance patrol," says Clayton, "and they couldn't see any men out here on the line at all. They weren't quite sure that it was occupied."

The Japanese didn't see soldiers, but they spotted laundry drying in the breeze. Disobeying orders to wait for reinforcements, their officer led his regiment straight to the socks and underwear.

"They got up there and got to the ventilator shafts and were still undetected," Clayton says. "It was a complete surprise. And I can just imagine these fellows being in there. Some would be sleeping away. There might be a few of them sittin' up, shootin' the guff or somethin'. And these Japanese are outside. And then they started droppin' their grenades down into the shafts. It must have been an awful shock to these guys. And many a good Scotsman died down there."

Screams of hand-to-hand combat with bayonets, rifles and grenades echoed across the valley as the Japanese attacked the Gin Drinker's Line.

It had taken the British six years to build the line. It took the Japanese Imperial Army six hours to breach it. In the next two days, they overcame the British, pushing them into Kowloon, which was under daily air-raid attack. On December 11, four days after Pearl Harbor, the British commander of Hong Kong ordered the mainland evacuated. Commonwealth troops would try to hold the island until help arrived.

Without mental or technical preparation, the two Canadian battalions designated as unfit for combat were suddenly pitted against the Japanese army at the peak of its power. The Commonwealth troops, along with hundreds of thousands of Chinese, desperately tried to find passage over to Hong Kong island. Wounded, scared, startled by the strength of the Japanese attack, the Canadians scrambled down Nathan Road towards the Kowloon docks, retracing the steps they had so blithely taken just three weeks before. Their orders were: "Everything not portable must be destroyed." They smashed the engines and slit the tires on trucks they left behind, opened the warehouses to looters. The docks rocked with explosions. Overhead, bombers dove like shrieking vultures. Mothers screamed for their lost children; husbands, for their wives. The island of Hong Kong — and safety — lay less than a mile across the strait.

"Bedlam," recalls one private. "Everyone trying to get a boat. Prices crazy. Looters being shot all around us. One sergeant, giggling happily, was shooting at anyone, looter or not, as long as he was a coolie. Good clean fun. One guard at a warehouse was letting looters inside, then shooting them down. We took a ferry at gunpoint."

In the panic of the following days, some soldiers slipped away for one last fling:

"My company was moving out over to the island of Hong Kong but I decided I wasn't going to go over there," says Bert Delbridge, a Grenadier private. "I wanted to go where the action was. So I took off and went a different way. We went downtown and sat in a bar and got drunk. What the hell. We weren't interested in it. And of course, you know the usual thing the Canadian soldier does, look for girls. We found them and we had a good time."

Most of them made it eventually to the island. A few, like John Gray, didn't. Tied to a lamp-post at the Star Ferry Wharf in Kowloon, shot dead at 21, he became a footnote to history: the first Canadian soldier killed in the first wave of the Japanese invasion of Hong Kong.

A NOTE OF SURRENDER.

Whoever surrenders with this note will be assured by the Japanese Army of his prompt return to the former life of peace and love.

Japanese Commander.

This surrenderer should be treated kindly.

此ノ投降人ハ懇切ニ後送スベシ

Japanese Commander.

軍 司 令 官

A Japanese surrender note dropped from the air during the Battle of Hong Kong.

THE SIEGE

At dawn, December 12, the last of the civilian and Commonwealth troops crossed from Kowloon to the island, the Japanese at their heels. From the island, Clayton could hear the carnage in Kowloon:

"It was horrible. The screams and ... all night long was just ... I don't know what they were doin' when they got in there. I guess they were looting and everything else. But that whole city was just one massive scream all night long. Just raised the hair on the back of your head."

For the next week, the Japanese flew daily raids over the island of Hong Kong, bombing and strafing anything that moved on the streets of Victoria and in the hills. The purpose of the raids was two-fold: to destroy enemy installations and to demoralize the civilian population. The

A Japanese propaganda leaflet addressed to the East Indian soldiers.

A propaganda leaflet aimed at the Chinese population of Hong Kong.

raids continued into the nights.

Having demonstrated their military superiority, the Japanese dispatched a peace mission to the island, demanding that the British surrender or be annihilated. Within 15 minutes, the ultimatum received a one-word reply — "No!"

The Japanese met the Commonwealth defiance with a ferocious artillery barrage. They knew the positions of the pillboxes and coastal guns and fired with deadly accuracy. First-aid posts filled with savagely wounded.

The haunting voice of Vera Lynn — "We'll meet again, don't know where, don't know when" — drifted over Victoria from a Japanese loudspeaker on Kowloon wharf. Between

Lye Mun Passage, the most vulnerable approach to the island of Hong Kong from the mainland.

shelling barrages and Vera Lynn, the Japanese broadcast Christmas propaganda messages designed to demoralize the defending troops even further. Leaflets rained down on the city and hillsides, exhorting Chinese civilians and Indian troops to revolt against their "British masters."

For the next five days the Japanese threw everything they had at the island, softening it up for the coming amphibious assault. In Victoria, the capital, all was chaos. Many of the Chinese, knowing that an invasion was imminent, deserted their posts on gun emplacements and in hospitals. Gangs of armed Chinese youths roamed the island, looting homes and stores and robbing civilians. A dusk-to-dawn curfew was imposed.

The British commanders still believed that the Japanese attack on the island of Hong Kong would come from the south, not from the mainland.

With all 14,000 troops on the island, the British reorganized their defences. Grenadiers, including the 100 men in Bob Manchester's D company, were sent to man the Wong Nei Chong Gap.

The most vulnerable point of the island was the northeast corner, where only a third of a mile of water separates it from a finger of mainland known as Lye Mun. Having taken

Walter Jenkins, 21, from Souris, Manitoba.

Kowloon, the Japanese had moved east and massed their powerful units at the narrow isthmus.

Bob Clayton and others from The Royal Rifles were put under the command of a British officer, and moved opposite Lye Mun to guard the east side of the island.

On December 18, 1941, the night was black, the moon obscured by rain clouds, the air thick with smoke from the bombed, blazing Anglo-Persian oil refinery. At 10 p.m., under cover of darkness, 3,500 Japanese soldiers embarked from Lye Mun on junks, sampans, rafts, dinghies — anything that would float — and swarmed onto the island of Hong Kong. A second assault force of 4,000 men followed at midnight. Within hours of landing, the Japanese controlled the bulk of the island's northeast coast.

All the Canadians, even non-combatants, were pressed into service. "Everyone got the wind up," remembers Walter Jenkins, a labourer from Souris, Manitoba. "'Hey, the Japs are comin' down the road.' This is the main road in Hong Kong, right. Everybody gets out. They're behind the sandbags, right. I said to the sergeant — always an efficient sergeant around there — I says,

"'Hey, I haven't got a sandbag.'

"'Ah, don't worry about it; it'll just get in your way.'

"And I'm thinkin', 'Well, that's what I want the fuckin' thing for!'"

Entrenched 60 feet underground at Fortress Headquarters on the southeast edge of the island, the British commanders dismissed reports that the Japanese had landed. In the jungle, John Stroud knew otherwise.

"It was dark. And we heard someone coming. But he said, 'Don't worry. It's me, Joe.' And then he lunged and thrust his bayonet into my leg. It was a Jap, but he had said, 'It's me, Joe,' in perfect English. Not even an accent. And then the Japanese were all over us."

A little after midnight, Bob Clayton was ordered to get flare pistols from the storage warehouse near the Lye Mun barracks. He left his unit struggling to hold the main road leading to Stanley and made his way down Sai Wan Hill.

"Then, I'm coming back up the road and the Japanese bowled this here hand grenade down the road. All of a sudden a sheet of flames comes up and hits me right in the face and I spin three times. When I spin, I have a flash of that scene in *All Quiet on the Western Front,* where the shell lit up in front of

Remains of Lye Mun West Battery, near where "Flash" Clayton was wounded.

the soldier and he spins. That's what I thought when I was spinning, and down I went.

"Well, I couldn't hear anything, with a concussion and everything. Jack told me after, in prison camp, that when I went down these three Japanese came out of the side of the ditch and they come up the road screaming and hollering with their bayonets. He could see them because we'd been watching them after they landed. And down in the city was a fire from the shelled rubber factory. I was outlined in that. So these three Japs come tearing out. Lorne Latimer and Jack killed these three Japanese.

"I crawled up the road and was hollering for my platoon officer, Kevin Strang. And he says, 'Did you get flare pistols?' And I says, 'No sir, I couldn't get in to get the flare pistols.' I told him the door was locked and I didn't want to make too much noise 'cause I could hear the Japs. And when I come back up the road that's when I got hit. So he says, 'You'll have to go back again.' I said, 'I can't go back again, I've been hit and I can't walk.'

"So he picked me up. He was a big man, about six-foot-four. He picked me up like a baby and carried me into this communications room. And Jack Ferrigan was in there. They sat me in a chair. So Jack says, 'Where ya hit, Flash?' And I says, 'I don't know.' So anyway, he cuts my pants off and I'd

Lieutenant Arthur Scott, 23, from Quebec City, Quebec, before leaving for Hong Kong with The Royal Rifles of Canada.

been hit in both legs. So, he's binding up my legs and all of a sudden I started to get cold and I guess I started to sway and of course this was shock and I didn't know it. They had a big container of rum there so he gave me a shot of rum. He bound up my wounds and put me on a bed where I could sleep.

"And then things got real hot outside. You could hear the bullets and everything else. And I said, 'Jesus, Jack, you'd better hand me that rifle in the corner there because those sons of bitches are going to get in here and I want to have something to fight with.' So he went ahead and passed it to me and the firing pin was busted. So I had two hand grenades on my chest. And this guy Lorne Latimer come in and he says, 'Holy Christ, Sarge, my Tommy gun's jammed. Can you fix it?' So I fixed it. Now, this Lorne Latimer, he got killed around the 23rd of December. And this is the truth, I remember saying to him, 'How's things going, Lorne,' and he said, 'I never had a better time in my goddamn life.'

"So a little later Lieutenant Scott comes in. He didn't know I'd been wounded. They'd come in there to find out what was going on. He says, 'Holy Jesus, Sarge, my bloody Tommy gun's jammed, can you fix it?' We had them round magazines in them which were shit. Always jamming. We got the boxed ones that they used after, they were good, but those round ones were murder. So I worked on that and got it fixed. And he went out the door.

"Then Lorne Latimer come in and said he was running out of grenades and asked me for mine. I said, 'Lorne, I'll give you one but I'm going to keep one, because I don't have anything to fight with. If they get in here, that's all I have.' So I gave him one of the grenades and kept the other one. Now it's getting kind of late — early morning, the 19th. The next thing, our Major's in, Major Bishop. And he's on the wireless talking to the colonel. And he says, 'Colonel Home, we got to get out of here. We're all dead men. The Japs are too strong up on the hill. We can't get them out of there.' We're down on the bottom, we've held them all this time.

"Oh, and he called before that. I have to mention this because I never saw such fireworks in my life. He called in artillery fire and there were 9.2s from Stanley, and when they hit the side of the hill, Holy Jesus, I don't know what it did to those Japs. Man, oh, man. You could just see the splinters going up the side of the hill. Because that's a gigantic shell. That saved us because that broke up the Japs, too.

A Canadian Army barracks at Lye Mun.

"Anyway, he calls Colonel Home. So the Colonel gave him permission to pull out. The next thing I hear is everybody going up the road and I thought, 'Holy Jesus, what's going to happen to me...'

"I'm still inside there, and I'm lying on the bed and I can't get up to lock the door, eh, because I can't walk. I'm alone. I'm all by myself, and they're gone. I must have laid there 15, 20 minutes, it seemed like 23 hours. So you get scared and you think funny. And this is the truth. So I took the pin out of the hand grenade and I threw the bloody pin away. I thought, 'Okay, rather than they get me, I'll just put it here on my chest. I won't know what's going on anyway.' Then I'm talking to myself and say, 'Well that's the cowardly way to do it. I'll wait till they get in here then I'll put it up there, and at least I'll take some of them with me.'

"So I laid there and laid there and the next thing the door opens and in walks this Lieutenant Scott. He says, 'Sarge, I got a way up the road and I wondered where you were. I run into Bishop and asked him, where's Sergeant Clayton?'

"That man came back all the way down that road in the dark by himself. He put me on his back, and we started up the road and I said, 'I'll never forget this.' He said, 'Hey Sarge, we'll have a drink on it some day.' But we never got that drink together. They found him with three of our privates, all tied together and bayoneted. That's what happened to him.

"Anyway, he got me up the road and the first ones we ran into were Bishop and Lorne Latimer. They were right at the back with Tommy guns, covering everything. How they didn't shoot us, I don't know, 'cause it's still that black.

"Then, down came a British armoured car, and Scott pounded on the door, gets me in, and they ask me what happened. I said, 'I don't know.' I didn't know what I'd got hit with at that time. I didn't know whether it was a shell, a mortar, I didn't know. I said, 'I'm hit in both legs.'

"The Brits kind of had the wind up, saying, 'Watch it now, watch it, them Japs shouldn't be very far away.' And every once in a while they would fire with their machine gun and the hot, Jesus, spent shells were landing down on me. So we got up the road, near Mount Parker, that was where our headquarters were.

"There's this little room there where they're taking the wounded in, an officer there to look at you, a British medical officer to operate. And I'm on this stretcher. Well, he looked me over, did a few things with my legs. The next thing, I'm in an ambulance going down the road and somebody opens fire on the ambulance, knocked the front window out of it. I got wounded in the face, you know, with glass, and shrapnel.

"So we had to turn around and come back. We wind up back where we were before. Turned around and they sent an armed guard with us and now we wound up in St. Stephen's Hospital.

"I guess I was all covered in blood. And they brought me in and put the stretcher on the floor, or maybe it was a bed, I don't know. And this lady come over, she was a volunteer nurse. I guess she'd be 40 years old. And she come over and knelt down beside me and looked at me. And I'll never forget the look on her face. I can just never forget it. It was like she was saying, 'Boy, oh boy, what's this kid doing here.' Then she went away, and she come back with a bucket of water, or a pail of water, whatever it was, and washed my face all off. Washed my legs all off. And asked me if there's anything that I'd like. And I said I'd like to have a hot chocolate if they had any. So she went and got me a hot chocolate ... she got me hot chocolate ... Then she said, 'You try to go to sleep now.'"

WONG NEI CHONG GAP

By dawn, when British headquarters finally accepted the reality of the Japanese attack, the Japanese had landed 7,500 soldiers, forced The Royal Rifles back from Lye Mun and cracked straight up the mountain where The Winnipeg Grenadiers were astride the critical mountain pass. The Japanese were so close to Canadian headquarters that by noon Lawson had destroyed the brigade's cipher books and radioed Ottawa, "Situation very grave."

Wong Nei Chong Gap was still the only way through the centre of the island. To control Hong Kong, the Japanese would have to take the pass. Two Japanese infantry regiments — about 2,000 men — were assigned the task.

Facing the Japanese were 100 Grenadiers, including Bob Manchester. Around them, the green hills floated in the mist like a meditative scene in a Chinese watercolour. But the landscape did not stay serene for long.

"About three-thirty or four o'clock on the morning of the 22nd, all hell broke loose," says Manchester. "The Japs crawled along the top of the shelter and lobbed grenades down on us in fine style. Many of the men were already wounded and the exploding grenades had a most demoralizing effect. We could see those grenades in the dark, spitting and sparking before they exploded. We'd hung on for about four and a half days. And we were now running out of ammunition and food."

Bourbonnière, trying to make his way through the hills from the Gap to nearby Mount Nicholson where another fierce battle was underway, was hit:

"I was burning, numb. Jap sniper got me. It's all right, just lie quiet here for a while. Jap sniper come out to see if you die, if you got gold in your mouth. I'm waiting for him. I got a new magazine in my Sten. So I let him come. I let him come real close. I emptied it in his body. Made a big hole in him. But I wasn't satisfied; I tromped his head in. Oh! You couldn't believe the grudge you get after a while."

Manchester was hit as well. "The Japanese machine gun on top of the hill opened up again. And just at that time I got smacked in the arm. The marks on my forearm are still here — there are four holes that went through."

The Japanese outnumbered the defenders 20 to one, but the Japanese were taking four times as many casualties. The Canadians hung on until their ammunition was practically expended to the round.

"Never surrender," says Bourbonnière. "Well, that was the biggest mistake. Because a lot of our boys died. They were finding them maybe 10 days, 14 days after, they were still coming out of the hills. And some wouldn't give up. They fought till the end. They wouldn't give up to anybody. They wouldn't surrender. You're all scattered all over the place. Nothing was organized. You fight for yourself and you fight for your life. You just had to do the best you could, that's all. We didn't have a chance. We were just like a bunch of cattle being slaughtered."

And in one of history's less edifying ironies, it was Brigadier Lawson, the man who had declared these battalions unfit for battle, who led the desperate last stand of the Canadians at Wong Nei Chong Gap.

"There's been a lot of BS about how Lawson died," reports Manchester. "One version even had him charging out of his bunker with two pistols blazing, right out of the wild west. That's a crock. I was manning a gun not far away and saw him and three others run from the bunker and start up the hill. A Japanese machine gun firing at us suddenly switched over to them. They were just shot down like ten pins, like clay ducks."

After Lawson's death, the handful of men left alive surrendered. They had no food, no water, no ammunition. The bodies of their comrades lay bullet-ridden in the trenches.

Lawson's corpse wasn't left to rot in the sun, as were so many others. Colonel Toshishige, the commander of the Japanese regiment, recognized Lawson's particular brand of courage. "I ordered the temporary burial of the officer on the battleground where he had died so heroically," says Toshishige. "I ordered our medical units to help their wounded and give them biscuits, water and cigarettes."

"On the morning of the 23rd the Japanese moved us out," Manchester recalls. "All the walking wounded. They told us that the war was over as far as we were concerned. We asked about the wounded and could we take them with us, and they said, 'No. Definitely not. Leave them here; we'll take good care of them.' So they did — real good care. They went in and put bayonets in them, shot them, and then they burnt the whole works that were left."

The fight for Wong Nei Chong Gap had cost both sides dearly. Most of the 300 Canadians killed in Hong Kong were casualties of the Gap. The Japanese had lost 800 men and were left with a thirst to avenge the deaths.

Amid the carnage, however, there were gestures of humanity. The United Church Chaplain assigned to The Grenadiers was one of those captured at Wong Nei Chong Gap on the morning of December 22. When his captors pushed him into a rain ditch, he thought he would die. But a Japanese officer pulled him out, marched him safely past two groups of soldiers who raised their rifles to shoot and knelt with him at the top of a hill.

"While we knelt together he surveyed the distant hillside through his field glasses," the Chaplain remembers. "He turned to me and then pointed to the hills, putting his hands to his eyes and face. I interpreted this to mean that across the valley were men with my colour of face and type of eyes.

"Apparently he was satisfied with my interpretation, for immediately he pointed down the hillside and indicated that I was free to go. I felt very grateful for his attention and was convinced that not only was I being given a chance, but my men left behind would also be saved. I wanted to show my appreciation so gave my best smile and heartiest handshake and said, 'Thank you' in my best English. He understood this gesture. His handshake was firm, and he smiled as if to say, 'The best of luck.'"

The Chaplain made his way down through Happy Valley towards the harbour of Hong Kong. Eventually, disguised as a Chinese, he reached the Hong Kong naval hospital in Victoria.

Chinese men, women and children, their possessions on their backs, poured from the hills into the city, where the remaining British and Canadian troops were digging in for the final siege.

Churchill's rhetoric was now in full wartime sail. From faraway England, he sent a defiant message to the beleaguered defenders of the tiny island colony: "There must be no thought of surrender.... Every day that you are able to maintain resistance you help the Allied cause around the world and by a prolonged resistance you and your men can win the lasting honour which we are sure will be your due."

With superb military orchestration, the Japanese had destroyed the puny Hong Kong air force before it had a chance to take off. They had wiped out its antiquated navy, cut off the island's water supplies and split the defending force in half by driving a wedge through the centre of the island. The defenders, their backs to the sea, were all but vanquished in a one-sided battle

Victorious Japanese soldiers parade through Kowloon.

that had lasted only 18 days. The corpses of 1,600 Commonwealth soldiers, including 303 Canadians, lay on the beaches and in the rugged mountains and valley passes of Hong Kong.

THE BRITISH SURRENDER

The wounded Canadian soldiers were evacuated to St. Stephen's College outside Stanley, a British-style private school for the children of wealthy Hong Kong Chinese. The school had been transformed into a temporary field hospital staffed by 2 doctors and 11 nurses. On the gleaming hardwood floors of the library lay 93 badly wounded soldiers.

This is where Bob Clayton was brought two days before Christmas, 1941. The grenade that exploded between his legs had rendered him incapable of walking. Confined to his bed, he would witness the horror of war — when all that is decent and dear is obliterated and what remains is vicious and bestial. Inexpressible horror.

It would be, even for those who lived through it, forever beyond comprehension.

Clayton lay among the wounded, the dead and the dying,

St. Stephen's College, a private school for the children of wealthy Hong Kong Chinese, became a hospital during the Battle of Hong Kong.

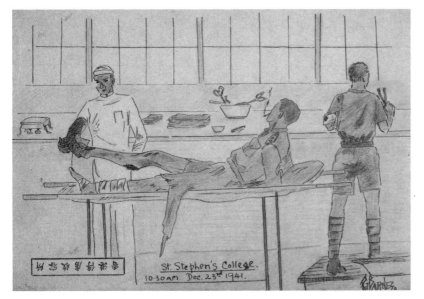

Hong Kong native, R.V. Barnes, was an orderly at St. Stephen's when he sketched wounded Donald Languedoc.

desperately wishing for the sweet relief of sleep. But the hospital, its Red Cross flag flying, was under constant shell bombardment: the noise was relentless. With his eyes wide open, Clayton listened to the machine-gun fire of the approaching Japanese; through the eerie light of hurricane lamps, he watched the staff move resolutely from bed to bed, trying to calm and comfort the wounded. A Canadian chaplain suggested evacuating the most serious cases, but the British officers refused. In fact, there was no place to evacuate them to. The Japanese controlled the centre of the island and had pushed the Commonwealth troops to Victoria in the west and Stanley in the east.

At 5:30 a.m. on Christmas Day, 200 Japanese attacked St.

Kay Christie, 30, from Toronto,
Ontario, a nurse with the Canadian
Army in Hong Kong, cared for
survivors of the St. Stephen's
massacre.

Stephen's. In his bed above the auditorium, Clayton could
hear them coming.

"The Japs started to come down, and our fire started to peter
out as the guys got overrun and killed. There was a helluva
commotion outside. And I heard somebody holler, 'For Christ
sake, hold on, don't let those bastards get in this hospital!'
When the Japanese came through the door, the doctors met
them and they had their hands up."

About 200 Japanese soldiers — some intoxicated by the
Bushido Code that promised them deification after death,
some drunk after breaking into a nearby distillery, others filled
with hatred and vengeance for losses suffered at Wong Nei
Chong Gap — crashed through the front door of St. Stephen's.

"They slaughtered everybody downstairs," Clayton reports.
"The doctors tried to surrender the hospital, and they
bayoneted them and killed them. And then they killed the
other guys downstairs. I could hear this going on. Then, the
next thing, they're upstairs and got us."

The surviving nurses and wounded soldiers, among them
Clayton, were dragged down the corridor into the school's
dormitory.

"This Jap come through the door and he's looking around,"
Clayton recalls. "And sittin' right beside the door, just inside
the door, was a Royal Scot. And he had six machine-gun
bullets in his arm. Soon as that Jap saw him, he took off his
steel helmet and he was roarin' and screamin' and hollerin'
and was pounding at that Royal Scot's arm. Then he looked
around a little more and he just pointed to some guy and out
the door he went with the fella."

One after the other, soldiers were taken out, tortured and
dismembered with swords, the corpses thrown one on top of
the other. Atop this human mattress, the raping of the nurses
began.

Four Royal Rifles were brought in as witnesses. The
Japanese commander cut out the tongue of one soldier and ears
off another. He told the witnesses, "Go to Fort Stanley and tell
your officers what you have seen. Hong Kong must surrender
or all prisoners will be killed in this way."

Laurie MacKay, a bullet in his neck, watched from his cot as
the Japanese soldiers started killing around him. MacKay had
dropped out of school in Truro, Nova Scotia, to join the army;
he was now just 17.

"I said, 'Oh my God — this is it.' I pulled the blankets over
my head. One Jap run over me to bayonet the guy in the next

bed. I rolled off my mattress and made a run for the door. I was hit over the head and went arse over teakettle. Don't remember a thing till I came to and this Red Cross nurse was trying to stop this Japanese soldier from killing us. So the soldier grabs her by the throat and drags her away.

"They kept coming back to the room and firing into it. The fear had really set into me. I had my head down, and this old First World War vet says to me, 'Look kid, we're going to die today. But one thing we're going to do, we're going to die like Canadians. Don't be scared of them.'

"Then this Jap soldier came in. He says, 'Canada!' And I says, 'Yeah. The hell with you. Go ahead, you bastard, kill me.' He looks at me and starts kicking me. And then he says, 'Canada! Cowboy?' And I says to myself, what's going on here. So I says, 'Yeah, cowboy.' So he steps back, and he twirls his hand over his head like a lariat and he yells, 'Whooee — ouw, ouw, ouw, yip, yip, yip!' And then he tells me to stand up. 'Quick draw!' And all night he kept bringing back his friends and tellin' me, 'Quick draw!'

"Then later he brings me a pack of cigarettes. A picture of Deanna Durbin. And an alarm clock. The cigarettes I really appreciated. The alarm clock I didn't know how long I was going to need. And the picture of Deanna Durbin? Well, I guess they knew she was Canadian too."

The woman who had nursed MacKay was raped, then killed.

Laurie MacKay, 16, from Truro, Nova Scotia, with his niece and nephew, soon after joining up.

"It was Christmas Day," Clayton continues, "and naturally you're thinkin' about Christmas and you're thinkin' about home, and I thought of my mother a million times. And I knew she'd be goin' crazy; absolutely crazy. Which I found out after was true.... Anyway, you do stupid things. And sittin' there on the floor, I kept saying, 'Ma, I'm all right. Ma, I'm all right.'"

The Japanese killed seven nurses after the gang rape. Of 95 wounded soldiers, 63 died.

Outside, the British commander ordered The Royal Rifles to retake Stanley. Outnumbered ten to one, The Rifles said it was suicide. The commander insisted. On Christmas afternoon, Clayton's friends attacked, fought a futile, vicious battle and were annihilated. "Jackie Lyons, Henry's brother, died down there. Latimer died down there..."

Scores of Japanese soldiers were killed, too, in the desperate hand-to-hand combat.

"Later on, when I looked out here, the Japanese had all their dead lined up," says Clayton, "and they were all in a row, like they were on parade. There were a lot of them. I wish there'd of been a hell of a lot more. They had like pink cloths over their heads, so you couldn't see their faces. And I guess it must have been their grave or registration number on it. An officer, or whoever it was, was going along and markin' all the names down." That afternoon, with Victoria about to fall, the British commander finally realized that further resistance was useless. At 3:15 p.m. on Christmas Day, he officially surrendered to the forces of the Emperor.

Across the colony, the Union Jack was lowered and the Rising Sun was raised. Unaware of the surrender, many Canadians fought on in the hills while in full regalia, astride a white stallion, the Japanese commander paraded in triumph through the streets of Victoria.

The last defenders of Hong Kong, 12,000 British, Indian and Canadian soldiers, were now prisoners of war. Some appeared almost jovial, happy at least to have survived. Many expected to be treated civilly, according to the rules of the Geneva Convention. Over the next three and a half years of detention, in the unfolding and unpredictable horror of war, many of the living would come to envy the dead.

SHAM SHUI PO PRISON CAMP

The Canadian survivors of the Battle of Hong Kong, about 1,672 in all, included Manchester and Bourbonnière, captured at Wong Nei Chong, and Clayton, captured at St. Stephen's Hospital. The men were herded into prisoner of war camps at North Point on the island and at Sham Shui Po on the mainland.

Exhausted and scared, they huddled in their new quarters — bullet-scarred, vermin-infested huts. Some slept on wood-plank double bunks, others on cement floors. There was no heat. Through the frigid January nights, they crouched around tins with strings soaked in peanut oil. Staring into the tiny flame, the country boys imagined blazing fireplaces and cozy woodstoves 3,000 miles away. During the day, the POWs left the barracks to roam the camp, digging up clumps of earth and grass to eat. As winter turned to summer, they exchanged tattered uniforms for a kind of thin cloth diaper. Some sat

Donald Languedoc, 26, from Montreal, Quebec, kept a scrapbook throughout his imprisonment.

Sham Shui Po, the largest POW camp in Hong Kong.

desolate, blank-eyed. Others took to compiling recipe books of favourite dishes, trading their fantasies like mad gastronomes. A few wrote diaries, and Royal Rifles Lieutenant Don Languedoc secretly kept a scrapbook filled with recollections and sketches of daily life in the camp.

Twice a day, the prisoners were counted. One after another, they reeled off their camp numbers in Japanese. *Ich, ni, san, shi, go, lock, nana, hachi, cue, ju...*

Now the Canadians pressed their faces against the fence, thrusting their hands through the barbed wire to beg food from Chinese passers-by, just as the Chinese had begged from them less than two months before.

When foraging parties were finally allowed out of the camps, they brought back books and set up a camp library — crime books, romances, politics, Freud. They did what they could to stay alive. Most hoped they would be released before the mosquitoes hatched.

"The first eight months, we were looking for Chiang Kai-shek over the hills every day," says Bourbonnière. "'Oh yeah, he's supposed to be here this afternoon,' we would say. 'Oh, I don't know how many thousand troops...'"

But the Canadian POWs would see four long winters before

Starved POWs watching a sunset, rendered by Lieutenant A.V. Skyorzov, an inmate of Sham Shui Po, who faithfully recorded conditions at the camps.

they saw home. Over 200 would never return at all.

Bourbonnière was one of the survivors. He struggled to help his older brother through the ordeal.

"When they took us to the camp from the hospital, they told us to take all we could carry. So I've got this big hospital mattress. They're heavy. I got sheets, pillows, oh, and these soup bowls. I'm thinking of my brother. I don't even know if he's alive. But I carried this mattress into camp because if he hasn't got one, I can always split the mattress in half and make a double bed for both of us. I must have carried that three miles at least.

"Anyway, I found my brother in there. I was glad to see him. He wasn't wounded at all, but he had no bed. So I told him I got this mattress, and he could share it with me. But he was the oldest of the family. I was the youngest. And he always figured I tried to boss him around. So I want him to move into my hut. I begged him to come and live with me. No, he wouldn't come stay with me. I said, 'Come on.' I brought utensils for him too. So he comes for a couple of weeks, and then he gets mad and takes off. Then he sells his bowl for cigarettes. Oh, I was mad. He sold that bowl for cigarettes. And he'd sell his rice and stuff like that.

The prisoner beside the wire fence at the Sham Shui Po waterfront wears a "pandoohi," the only garment distributed free to inmates. Soldiers saved the remains of their uniforms for muster parades and times when the Japanese demanded proper dress.

A Japanese sentry takes night count at Sham Shui Po officers' barracks. Each prisoner was responsible for a group of his friends and one man in each hut reported the numbers present.

"Soon he got dysentery and malnutrition. He got all crippled up with sores and he was laying in the corner of a hut in water. I moved him out of there. He got electric feet. And he was all bloated with beriberi, swollen up. He was leaning against a board in this little hospital we had in the camp. A little hospital with no beds or nothing. He was too swollen to lie down. He was finished. So I jumped the fence. I gave a

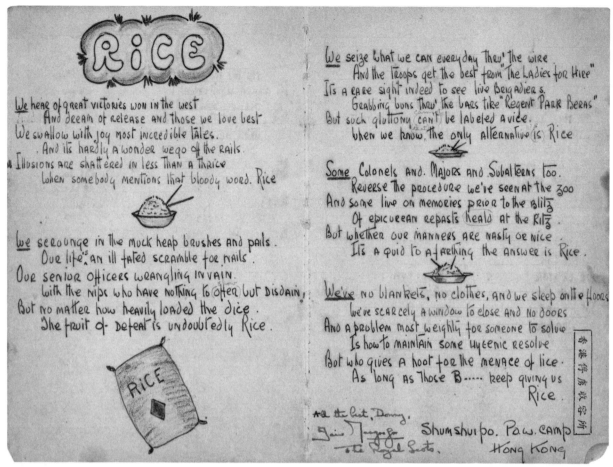

An ode to rice, by an anonymous POW.

military shirt to some Chinese for powdered soybean milk. I got back into the camp and I sneaked back into where he was and I mixed the powder with water in a can. I wanted him to drink it. But he'd given up. He wouldn't do it. So I grabbed him by the collar and I said, 'You drink this or I'll finish you off myself.' I shoved it. He gagged and everything. I poured it into him. And then I left. I figured he'd never live because he'd given up.

"The boys that were in the hospital with him, suffering from the same disease, they told me after I poured the soybean milk into him, he lost 14 or 15 pounds overnight; water going out of his system. Anyway, you know where I saw him again? In San Francisco I told the boys not to tell him I was alive. On the train going back to Canada, we got him pretty loaded." It wasn't until they were in Vancouver that Bourbonnière revealed his identity. "I said, 'Would you like to meet your brother?' He said, 'Is he alive?' I said 'Yes, I'm your brother.' But I was young, you see. I had changed a lot. When I took off my hat, he started to cry."

Despite the meagre rations — too often, only a handful of rice — the POWs were soon pressed into the service of the Empire of the Rising Sun.

"They decided that there was no sense in wasting good manpower, that these lazy buggers had better find something to do," recalls Manchester. "They decided they were going to enlarge their international airport. And so, they shipped us over there in work details at seven in the morning. And we'd stay over there until six at night."

"We chopped down bloody mountains with pick and shovel and a wheelbarrow. We had our breakfast before we went — some kind of punky rice and fish head soup or something. We'd have to take a goddamn can or anything we were able to accumulate to carry our lunch for our midday meal. An old bottle or whatever. And it was generally the rice and the soup all mixed together or seaweed. Then we'd get out there and have our lunch out there and then we'd have to come back. And we'd get the same old crap when we got back into camp."

Compelled by the threat of starvation, the prisoners began to build the runway, sabotaging the construction by over-mixing sand in the concrete to make the tarmac weak. It worked. The first Japanese aircraft to use the runway, a large fighter escort filled with dignitaries, crashed on landing. The Japanese engineer in charge of the project was decapitated. It was a sad victory in a long defeat.

Ironically, the torment of the POWs was exacerbated by another Canadian, Kanao Inouye, a native of Kamloops, British Columbia, who secretly left home and enlisted as an interpreter in the Japanese army. Nicknamed the "Kamloops Kid," Inouye took pleasure in beating Canadian prisoners within an inch of their lives. Clayton's tone turns bitter when he recalls his first encounter with the Kamloops Kid:

"We were lined up, and all of a sudden this son of a bitch comes along. He's walkin' up and down, and we're lookin' at this guy, you know. He's somethin' new, we never seen him before. So he stops and says, 'So, you're the Canadians, eh.' Just like that. Well, Jesus, we're really lookin' at this guy now. He says, 'I want you to know I was born and raised in Kamloops, B.C., and I hate your goddamn guts.' And he says when he was a kid and growin' up there, they'd call him 'little yellow bastard' and stuff like this. He never forgot that."

So bad was the camp that many prisoners became obsessed with escape. In late summer, 1942, four Grenadiers planned their flight from Sham Shui Po. Among them was John Payne, a 21-year-old artist-soldier who could carve a chess set out of

Kanao Inouye, the "Kamloops Kid," never forgot the taunts he suffered from Canadian kids back home in British Columbia.

John Payne, 21, from Winnipeg, Manitoba, on the day of his departure for Hong Kong.

"Mugs," was John Payne's nickname for his childhood sweetheart, Magdalene Lizotte.

mahogany and ivory as skillfully as he trained soldiers to fire a rifle. Payne was the offspring of a First World War love story. Ben, a British corporal, had won the hand of Margaret, a nursing sister, and emigrated with her to Canada to raise four children. Payne, the eldest, wrote beautiful letters home — to his mother and to his childhood sweetheart, Magdalene Lizotte, "Mugs."

Dear Mugs,

Sometimes I don't think you appreciate the work I've been doing for the British Empire to preserve Peace and Democracy on the Earth for many a year to come. It's always been like this. They laughed at Columbus, poisoned Socrates and the army cooks are trying to poison me. That's the thanks I get.

I'm in the same mood Homer must have been starting the Odyssey, but don't be alarmed; I'm not half the windbag he was....

The day before his escape attempt, Payne wrote a final note to his mother, with a postscript to his two sisters and his 14-year-old brother, Ben. He entrusted the letter to Bob Manchester.

Dear Mater:

I have decided, either fortunately or unfortunately as the case may be, to take a chance on getting through to Chungking. I've investigated as much as possible and I feel sure we stand a jolly good chance of getting there. There are numerous reasons for this step, the chief being that the cholera season and fly season is starting. Dysentery and Beriberi are high in Camp, and anyway, I'm ruddy sick of Japanese hospitality.

You share, I know, my own views on fatalism, so for that reason I know you won't condemn my judgment. So just in case I shouldn't make it, you must remember that according to our beliefs I have departed for a much nicer place (I hope) although it will grieve me to exchange the guitar for a harp even though there is a higher percentage of gold in the latter. But that's enough of this drivel, I'll be able to destroy this note myself, I'm sure, so bye-bye for now...

Your devoted son, John

P.S. Best regards to Di and Yvonne. Tell Ben to join the Air Force next war.

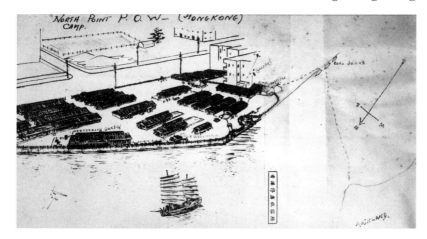

John Payne's drawing of his escape plan, submitted as evidence in the war crime trials following the war.

> 19. 8. 42.
> North Point Camp
> China.
>
> Dear Mater:
>
> I have decided, either fortunately or unfortunately as the case may be, to take a chance on getting through to Chungking. I've investigated as much as possible and feel sure we stand a jolly good chance of getting there. There are numerous reasons for this step the cheif being that the Cholera season + fly season is starting, Dysentery + Beri Beri are high in Camp, and anyway I'm ruddy sick of Japanese hospitality.
>
> You share, I know, my own views on fatalism, so for that reason I know you won't condemn my judgment. So just in case I shouldn't make it you must remember that according to our beliefs I have departed for a much nicer place (I hope) although it will grieve me to exchange the Guitar for a harp even though there is a higher percentage of gold in the latter. But that's enough of this drivel, I'll be able to destroy this note myself I'm sure so bye bye for now ...
>
> Your devoted Son
> John
>
> P.S. Best regards to Di + Yvonne. Tell Bert to join the Air force next war.

John Payne's last letter to his mother, protected through the war by Bob Manchester and delivered to Payne's family in October, 1945.

The four POWs scaled the wire and stole a sampan to cross the bay. The boat capsized and they were captured. Although according to international law, the maximum sentence for an escape attempt was 30 days detention, John Payne and the other three were brought to King's Park soccer field, tortured and decapitated.

It would be three more years before Manchester could deliver the folded scrap of paper that he kept safe and hidden through the hardships still to come. And it would be forever before John Payne's mother accepted his death.

SLAVE LABOUR IN JAPAN

In the fall of 1942, POWs at Sham Shui Po were given a chance to leave the camp to work in Japan, mining coal and making steel for the war against the Allies. Many volunteered, believing that even hard labour would be better than the disease and deprivation of the camps in Hong Kong. Their guards would be civilians, more civilized, they hoped, than soldiers. Surely nothing could be worse than Sham Shui Po.

"Then they used Chinese coolies to get their goddamned airport built," says Manchester, "and what happened after I left God only knows. But the stories that were told were that the boys who continued at Sham Shui Po had days of agony and nothing to do but sit around and contemplate their navel and starve themselves to death. That's about the size of it."

The first shipload of POWs bound for Japan left Hong Kong on October 1, 1942, and was torpedoed 70 miles south of Shanghai by an American submarine. In the two days it took the ship to sink, the 2,000 Japanese soldiers aboard were rescued from the deck. The 870 British POWs, locked in the holds, drowned.

Bob Clayton was in the first draft of 1,200 Canadian POWs shipped to Japan:

"We were marched on board the ship in Hong Kong and down into the hold. They crammed as many of us down there as they could. And when I mean down in the hold, I mean down in the hold. All there was, was the bottom deck, that's where we were. It took us three, four, five days, I'm not sure, lying on steel in the hold. And you're shitting in buckets and pulling it up in the morning. And then your food's coming down in buckets.

"When we docked, and they brought us out of the hold, we must have been something else. We couldn't smell each other because we were down there. But when we came up, them buggers were up on the top deck with their hands over their noses. And I was lookin' at them and thinkin', 'Well, we'll have our day.'"

John Stroud, 22 years old, describes being marched through

the streets of Kobe, near Osaka:

"All the Japanese pointing at us, you know, 'the conquered.' The mighty Japanese on their horses, shouting and yelling. We were herded into the Kobe station. There was a bombing raid on at the time, an air raid. But they didn't move us out; we stayed there. And we thought, 'What the hell, if we're going to get hit, we're going to get hit. At least we have a roof over our heads.'"

Manchester and Stroud were among the 500 POWs sent to the work camp at Niigata, an industrial port 250 miles northwest of Tokyo.

John Stroud at age 20, before going to Hong Kong.

"They said we would be better housed and better fed," says Manchester. "We wouldn't be worked as hard as when we were working on the airport runway. So we assumed, okay, this is what they're saying, this must be true. But it was a shit of a camp. Because of the type of work we had to do and the brutality of the camp staff and the weather, we lost more men than all of the rest of the work camps put together."

Manchester loaded coal, while other Canadian and British prisoners worked old mines, reopened to feed the battleships and factories of the Japanese war machine. If Hong Kong was purgatory, this was hell. The work was dirty, dangerous and often dragged on for 15 to 16 hours a day.

"The weather killed us more than anything," reports Manchester. "When we arrived it was in late September, early October. And then the winter set in, and in the middle of November, the snow came. We had seven foot of snow. The Japanese provided us with heavy matted grass capes to help ward off the cold and dampness on our backs. But they were more of a hindrance than a help, because they became thoroughly soaked and they weighted you down. The snow was so heavy that it crushed one of our shacks. That's where we lost 16 men on New Year's Eve, 1944."

"I'll tell you how we used to sleep," remembers Bourbonnière. "We matched two and two together. So you wouldn't freeze to death. One would sleep for a few hours. You wake him up, and then you'd sleep. So we saved ourselves. One boy died, the third one from me in the camp. I think it was Caruso; he died. Froze to death right in the camp lying there at night. His partner went to sleep and never woke him up."

The cold was murderous and the food was no better than the POW camp at Sham Shui Po. Characteristically, Bourbonnière was resourceful.

Fred Reich, working as a slave labourer at the Sendai coal mine, northern Japan, August, 1944.

"We asked our medical officer if we could cook some rats. He kind of laughed and said if you boil them for three or four hours, you'll boil the poison out of them. If you want to eat them, eat them. So me and my friends, we caught 22 rats. And they were big; just like cats. We stole a little wood at the foundry, a couple pieces at a time. And hid it in the camp. We asked our officer to ask the Jap if we could make a little fire, you know, at Christmas, the few days we were off. They granted us that much anyway.

"So we cooked our rats. And then we took the meat, eating it and the juice, the fat. So we figure we got protein. We drink the juice — hey, vitamins. We were like a bunch of kids. So the next day we went to work, and were we sick! Every two minutes we got to go to the lavatory. We got diarrhea, you could believe it. We never had any meat of any kind for two years. Nothing. When I went in there I weighed about 195, 200. Then I weighed about 117. And then drink this juice and that meat. We nearly died, the three of us. We couldn't walk... But they were good, those rats. Just like chicken."

Bob Clayton ended up working the coal mines. Like the other POWs, he found that hard work, bitter cold, disease and starvation were his real enemies.

"You worked three shifts in the mines. And when you come out of the midnight shift, say at eight in the morning, you had to go and work in the garden. We all shit in buckets and they kept it in a bigger bucket with a handle on it. Two of us would be on the big bucket of shit, and you had ladles, to ladle it out into the garden. Not manure, it was shit. Anyway, it was to grow potatoes and those potatoes never grew because we were eating the bloody potatoes and putting the tops back."

Clayton remembers diseases that most Canadians have never seen.

"We got Dip — diphtheria — which killed quite a few guys. And a lot of guys died of beriberi. First guy that died in my platoon was Clarence Wolbert and I went over to see him in the hospital. And he wanted to know how things were doing. I said, 'Jesus, good. The Chinese are coming; the Americans are coming.' And he said, 'They'd better hurry up.' And he threw back the cover, and his privates were as big as a melon, just from the wet beriberi. You could put your finger in your leg and your print would go in there and it would still be there two days later. You drowned in your own fluids from that.

"And we also had the dry beriberi — I had that. It's like somebody takes a knife and is shoving it in the bottom of your

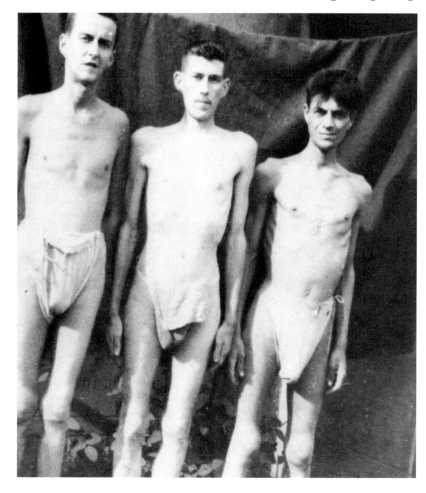

Leo Porterfield, Colin Standish and Donald McIver (left to right), photographed at Toyama POW camp, Japan, 1945.

feet. You know, you had hot feet all the time. You'd put your feet in buckets of cold water. And the feet started to rot and go bad, you know. So they had to cut that out. And things got so bad with the guys with the hot feet keepin' the other guys awake, they put them all in one ward. And we called it the Agony Ward."

"Noises of gurgling, choking, of men drowning, dying in diphtheria's bloody slime," wrote prisoner Bill Lee. "Those with beriberi clinging to slender life; faces grotesque, fat with water."

THE END OF THE STRUGGLE

On the night of March 10, 1945, at the shipyards in Yokohama, Bob Clayton looked up at the night sky and saw it suddenly explode.

"Everything lit up like, oh Jesus! I was sleeping with George Sofer and George says, 'Geez, I think we're going to get it tonight, Flash.' Outside, they had big pits, maybe 50 men would go in. They were like our air-raid shelters. So the next thing, the Japs are screaming and hollering, and we're all outside in the air-raid shelters. Holy Jesus, you could see those B-29s coming in real low.

"And they burnt that city of Yokohama down, which would be like burning down the city of Toronto. They burnt that whole thing down in one night, practically nothing left. And the people screaming outside, it was just...

"The thing that saved us, we were on the edge of the city. We were right beside a river and there was a bridge went over. And these people are running and hollering. They were trying to get away from the fire. Oh, all night was horrible. We went outside and we couldn't believe it. It was like standing in the west end of Toronto and looking east and it was gone. It was just gone."

For the Canadian POWs, it was a frightening first sign of possible release.

Five months later, on August 6, 1945, an American B-17 bomber dropped a 10.5-foot-long, 9,700-pound atomic bomb on Hiroshima. Nicknamed "Little Boy," it was the first atomic bomb used on a civilian population. It levelled the city, and its reverberations were felt throughout the world. Two days later, the Americans exploded another atomic bomb — this one with a force equivalent to 22,000 tons of TNT —on Nagasaki. The tremors reached the Canadian POWs in the coal shafts of Niigata, more than 500 miles away.

Emperor Hirohito surrendered. The broadcast of his surrender speech from the Imperial Palace was the first time that most Japanese had ever heard his voice. He exhorted them to learn to bear the unbearable. The enemy, Hirohito said, had developed a weapon so powerful that there was no other choice.

"We came up from the mine to the surface," recalls a Canadian POW. "The Japs had rigged loudspeakers to utility poles, and they made us sit around in a circle. And we heard this voice, this disembodied voice. I didn't understand what the hell he was saying. It was a sort of Japanese I couldn't understand. So one of the foremen interpreted for us and he said, 'That's the Emperor.'"

Bob Clayton will never forget his liberation from three and a half years of hell.

Haggard former Canadian POWs display the Japanese flag in Manila on their way home, 1945.

"One morning we get our lanterns to go to work. All the girls are crying. So I go down into the mine, wondering what's going on, and it's a different shift — nobody is getting a smash in the mouth, or anything. So we said, 'Jesus, you know, something must be going on.' Then, some of the bad buggers there disappear. And we're wondering, what the hell. And finally we find out, the bloody war is over.

"And after, we find out what happened. MacArthur broadcast to the Japanese, told them, 'Leave all the POWs alone. We're going to be dropping food, and don't you people touch it.' And then the Japs told us to put signs outside so our planes could find us. So we had to find something white and put it outside, on the four sides of the camp, way up in northern Japan. And I don't know how long it was ... you lose track of time. A week, two weeks, ten days? It doesn't matter, it's immaterial.

"One morning just after daybreak, Jesus, we hear these planes coming. And we're looking, and over they come. In a V, and I guess there were about 12 of them, and that's the way they come over, just like that. Fighter planes. And we're, Jesus, we're up like this, eh, we're in our underwear, we're crying and everything. And geez, away they go into the distance.

"A couple of minutes later they come back single file, all

Lieutenant-Commander Fred Day and another officer from the Canadian destroyer, The Prince Robert, liberating Canadian POWs, Sham Shui Po, August, 1945.

barrel-rolling over the camp. So shit, now we're all bawling, eh; we're all bawling. And then, I guess they designated a couple of them to come back. And they dropped us messages: put out this sign for this, this sign for that, if you got anybody dying, if anybody's attacking you. They had different signs to put out. And every couple of hours they'd come over and check on you. And they dropped us some cigarettes and some bread. They apologized and said, 'We're from an aircraft carrier. We don't have that much but we're dropping you what we can.' Every day they'd come over and check you."

The POWs, including Manchester, Bourbonnière and Clayton, were brought by train from the work camps of Niigata to American ships anchored in Tokyo Bay. Clayton recalls being met by a woman from the Red Cross.

"And she come up and talked to me, and I couldn't talk to her. I couldn't talk to her. She spoke to me and I couldn't speak to her. I had to turn away. Then, they had these troops lined up. Americans. And so I went up to thank this big SOB for getting me out of camp. And I couldn't talk to him. I started, and I filled all up, and I ... I turned around and I walked away. He must of thought I was crazy, or something. So then they take us in, spray us all, threw away the shit we had on and give us uniforms to put on. And the next thing we know ... it's early in the morning, it's eight o'clock."

Canadian POWs in Hong Kong at the time of their release.

Clayton and his fellow survivors were transported in small boats to the *Wisconsin*, a battleship carrying over 1,500 sailors. Hollow-eyed, jaundiced, they hardly had enough flesh to hold their skeletons together.

Five feet five inches tall, Clayton weighed 95 pounds.

Five feet eight inches tall, Friesen was 98 pounds.

Five feet ten inches, Bourbonnière weighed 85 pounds.

Five feet eleven inches, John Stroud was reduced to 79 pounds.

Six feet one inch, Bob Manchester was only 105 pounds.

"And they're looking down at us and we're looking at them," continues Clayton. "The next thing we're on the catwalk and we're on the deck. Then, this officer says, 'Line up.' The first time we ever heard a guy talk with a southern accent. So we all lined up, and we're looking bewildered. 'This is the last time you'll have to line up,' he says.

" 'You're the hungriest looking bastards I ever saw in my life. And we're going to do something about it right now.'

"The next thing, we're all sitting down at the tables, and so help me Christ, they must have served us with pitch forks. They're coming out with the eggs and the bacon ... well, we all wound up sick, we're puking over the side of the ship. Then they told us, 'Anytime you want to eat, *anytime* you want to eat on this ship, even if it's not mealtime, you don't have to worry. They just serve *us* at mealtime. But anytime *you* want to go downstairs, you just go into the cookhouse, and you tell that cook what you want. I don't care what it is, that cook will give it to ya.'"

THE AFTERMATH

The end of the war brought a settling of accounts. Allied forces began to round up Japanese soldiers accused of war crimes and bring them to trial. Many Canadians were asked to return overseas to take part in the trials, both as investigators and as witnesses.

One of the two nurses who survived the massacre at St. Stephen's Hospital was able to identify some of the Japanese soldiers responsible, and several were convicted of rape and murder.

Kanao Inouye, the Kamloops Kid who had tormented the POWs at Sham Shui Po, slipped out of the camp a few days before the liberation but was tracked down, captured, tried and convicted of war crimes. His lawyer appealed and had the conviction overturned on the grounds that Inouye was a Canadian citizen. Later, he was charged with high treason, found guilty and sentenced to hang.

Bob Manchester was one of those who returned to Japan to work on the Canadian War Crimes Commission. He lived for two years among the Japanese people. That experience, he says, saved his sanity.

"It took some of the edge off my bitterness. I began to understand a little more clearly the reasons behind war, and it wasn't the people themselves who were warriors. It was the industrialists and the warmongering senior officials of the military that created the problems, not the people on the street."

But the years of prison deprivation have taken their toll on the surviving 680 Hong Kong veterans. One recent study enumerates the many chronic illnesses intensified by the prison camp experience: 30 percent of Hong Kong vets suffer from deteriorating eyesight or blindness; 46 percent from psychological problems ranging from anxiety-caused sleep disturbance to psychosis; 50 percent from gastro-intestinal illness; and 50 percent from oral and dental ailments. Another study in 1965 concluded that, due in large part to prolonged malnutrition and vitamin deficiency, the death rate of Hong

Canadian veterans of Hong Kong sailing into Victoria, British Columbia, October 6, 1945.

Bob Manchester back home in Winnipeg, Manitoba, with his mother and his wife Edna, October, 1945.

Kong survivors is 24 percent higher than that of soldiers who fought in Europe.

Some of Canada's Hong Kong veterans ended the war with a burning hatred of the Japanese. Some resented the British officers who treated them badly. But many, like Clayton and Manchester, are even more furious with the Canadian government, which sent them on a desperately hopeless mission.

They offered their lives to their country, and entrusted their fate to their government. They felt that their trust was betrayed.

A royal commission, set up to investigate the circumstances

of Canada's involvement in Hong Kong, exonerated the Cabinet, the Department of National Defence and the senior members of the General Staff.

As veterans struggled with the psychological and physical aftermath of their long imprisonment, they also had to fight the federal government for medical and pension rights. Doctors from Veteran Affairs, ignorant of tropical diseases, accused the vets of malingering and dismissed the mental trauma of captivity. When the Hong Kong vets applied for Pacific Campaign benefits, the Department of National Defence awarded them $50 each.

In 1952, the Canadian government legally absolved Japan of any responsibility for wartime reparations to the Canadian survivors. In 1990, MP John Crosbie, representing the Mulroney Cabinet at Hirohito's funeral, declined to visit the cemetery where Canadian soldiers are buried.

In May, 1991, 46 years after the Canadians were released from the POW camps, Japan formally apologized to Canada for its harsh treatment of prisoners during the Second World War. "We feel very contrite about the unbearable sufferings and hardships," said Japanese Prime Minister Toshiki Kaifu.

Canada's prime minister, Brian Mulroney, considered the "statement of contrition" a most important one that would be noted "and I'm sure appreciated by the families affected." No mention was made of the Hong Kong veterans' claim filed three months earlier with the United Nations, asking that $20,000 in war reparations be awarded to each Japanese POW forced, against the Geneva Convention, to labour for free in Japanese war industries.

So distorted and suppresed is the Battle of Hong Kong that even the veterans have trouble bringing themselves to reveal what really happened.

"I didn't even tell my own mother everything," Clayton admits. "I never told her anything about the bad times or how it was in camp or anything else. I had ... Well, to tell you the truth I didn't want to talk about it too much. Even Lieutenant Scott that saved my life, I'm sorry to say I didn't write his wife and tell her what I thought of him until about two years ago."

Why did the friends of Clayton, Manchester and Bourbonnière have to die in the hills of Hong Kong?

How could human beings massacre the way they did at St.

Stephen's, or drop bombs on civilians the way they did at Hiroshima? Why did it take so long to tell the real story of Hong Kong?

Bob Manchester ponders the questions. His face contorts, he has nowhere to look. He shifts and turns and forces himself to make the attempt. "We tried to provide a reasonable explanation as to ... as to ..." His voice breaks. Tears roll down from the corners of his eyes.

Night Flights:
The Boys of
Bomber
Command

CHAPTER TWO

Canadian Ron Witts averted his eyes as the British Wing Commander ripped the sergeant's badge off his left sleeve. Witts was in the centre of a huge square formed by the 320 flyers and ground crew of Bomber Command's North Killingholme Station in Yorkshire, England. Around him, the reluctant witnesses shivered under their blue greatcoats in the February morning drizzle. They knew he had survived more than a dozen harrowing missions over Hitler's Germany. "There but for the grace of God..."

Witts was 19 years old. He had already flown 18 operations as a mid-upper gunner, strapped into the plastic turret atop a Lancaster bomber. Several nights earlier, on a bombing raid against a German submarine base at St-Nazaire, his Lancaster was trapped in the apex of six radar-directed searchlights. To escape the searing beams and the murderous flak that would inevitably follow, the pilot threw the plane into a rolling dive and lost control. The massive bomber flipped on its back and plummeted.

Pinned against his transparent turret, Witts watched the sea rush up to meet him — 17,000 feet, 15,000, 11,000 ... At 7,000 feet, the pilot pulled out of the terrifying dive. Something in Ron Witts snapped.

Half his buddies at Bomber Command had been killed or lost on missions. He had tried to forget his fear in mess hall antics and to drown his grief in the British pubs.

Ron Witts couldn't take it anymore. He told his commanding officer he wouldn't fly again.

But the Royal Air Force (RAF) had no sympathy for battle fatigue, only punishment for cowardice. The young gunner was publicly disgraced before his squadron and made an object lesson to the others. Within seconds, the decommission was effected; within minutes, the parade dismissed.

Ron Witts — his service record indelibly stamped "Lack of Moral Fibre" — was banished from the airfield. When he tells his story 50 years later, he hides his humiliation behind a pseudonym.

THE BOYS IN BLUE

For many young Canadians who wanted to fight in the Second World War, the Royal Canadian Air Force (RCAF) was the military command of choice. From their fathers and uncles, veterans of four long years of the First World War, they had heard about the gas attack at St-Julien, the face-to-face killing at Passchendaele and Vimy, the swamp of mud and blood that was the infantry. They did not want to go to the trenches. The place to be was above the carnage.

And flying was romantic. In the words of the pilot-poet, John Magee:

Oh, I have slipped the surly bonds of earth
And danced the skies on laughter-silvered wings;
Sunward I've climbed and joined the tumbling mirth...
Put out my hand, and touched the face of God.

Some recruits had paid a buck a ride to fly with the barnstormers, First World War vets who eked out a living during the Depression with their biplanes. Many had seen or heard of "Buzz" Beurling, the Montreal kid who had swept out hangars in exchange for flying lessons and had single-handedly shot down 27 German planes, practically winning the Battle of Malta. They watched spell-bound as Buzz, gaunt from dysentery and fatigue, did his Canada War Bond pitch:

"There was this one Italian plane, white, absolutely white. I got the pilot in my sights. He tried to turn, but I kept following him. I wanted this one particular shot. When I fired, I didn't hit the plane — but got the cockpit just like I wanted. One of my shells caught him right in the face and blew his head right off. It was a great sight, the red blood down the white fuselage."

Exigency heightened the romance. Britain had its back to the wall, with no land army to invade the Continent and a navy hard pressed to keep supply lanes open. The RAF, bolstered by Commonwealth boys, was England's only instrument of war against Germany. In less than a year, the Nazis had conquered all of Europe and forced the British off the beaches at Dunkirk. By the summer of 1940, Germans were poised across the Channel, demanding submission.

To help the war effort, Canada volunteered to be both an arsenal and a massive training ground for the British air force. Between 1940 and 1945, Canada built 15,000 war planes, two thirds of them training aircraft. And more than 200,000 fresh-faced young Canadian men and 17,000 women signed up with the RCAF. Fifty-eight flight schools graduated 1,500 air crew every month. Canada trained airmen from all over the British Commonwealth — 137,000 in all, more than England and the rest of the Commonwealth combined. Canada was the "aerodrome of democracy."

Doug Harvey wanted to join the RCAF from the moment he read the newspaper reports of Britain's first victory against the Luftwaffe.

"The *Telegram* and the *Star* were full of it — how the great German formations were bombing London and how our gallant fighters were roaring up to meet them and shoot them down. Pictures and exploits. The Battle of Britain heroes with their white scarves flying. It was just tremendous glamour. Glamour on top of the life I was leading in the Depression, locked in a dead-end reality. The air force was going to be the life for me."

Doug Harvey, 18, from Toronto, Ontario.

RCAF recruits in England.

Jim Moffat, 19, from Timmins, Ontario, soon after joining the RCAF.

Joseph Martin Favreau, 21, from Vaudreuil, Quebec, when he joined the RCAF.

At age 18, after two years working to help support the family, Harvey presented himself to a recruiting officer in Toronto, Ontario, and asked to be an air gunner.

"Why air gunner?" the officer said.

"Because I dropped out of high school. I don't think I have the education to be a pilot."

Harvey was offered a three-month night school course to bring his math up to Junior Matric level. He did it.

"Then they said, 'Okay, you can go for pilot.' So I did. Flying was such a thrill. Everyone wanted to be a fighter pilot.

"It was a black and white war. Hitler was running the world and we were gonna stop him. The guys with the white scarves, they saved Britain, and this was the outfit we were joining. The same spirit. The same dash."

At 19, Jim Moffat left his job in the mines and his family on the farm outside Timmins, Ontario, to fight Fascism on the Continent.

"My father was in the First World War and his outfit was blown up. He was burned and they thought he was dead. He was the sole survivor. He said if any of his family joined the service, he'd shoot them. And he was serious.

"But when war broke out, I tried to join the navy. I knew the names of almost every ship in every major navy. On the way down to enlist, I read in the paper that two corvettes sank and everyone survived except the poor stokers. And at the recruitment centre all they wanted was stokers."

Moffat went back to the mines where he worked on the elevator cages with his good friend, Roger Fournier. He had dated Roger's sister and liked to hang out at the Fournier house. When Roger signed up for the air force, Moffat did too.

"It was my duty to my country and my King. It's all baloney now but, then, it was really important. I remember that when I was out in gunnery school, the Russians started to turn back the Germans and I thought, 'I hope this war doesn't end before I can get over there.'"

Air crew recruits came from across Canada — the Yukon, the Maritimes, Quebec, Toronto, the Prairies, the Canadian west coast. Many recruits were of British descent, going to England to defend the Mother Country. Some came from the United States to join the RCAF, the world's fourth largest air force.

Martin Joseph Favreau, 21 years old from Vaudreuil, Quebec, 30 miles west of Montreal, was one of a thousand

French-speaking Canadians who joined up.

"I wasn't too happy with what the Germans were doing in Europe. I joined and was glad to defend my country. A lot of my friends said it wasn't our war. How could they say that when German submarines were sinking ships in the St. Lawrence River?

"In a war, it's the family and the land. We have to save those two. With land, you have family, and with family, you have a country."

AIRMEN IN TRAINING

It would be months before Moffat, Harvey, Favreau and the other Canadian recruits saw action. Successful air force applicants were trucked off to Initial Training School in Canada. There, they studied basic navigation and maths and were sorted into potential pilots, navigators, gunners, wireless operators. After graduation, the boys went to specialized schools. Ken Brown, a 22-year-old from Moose Jaw, Saskatchewan, and Doug Harvey went to Elementary Flying Training School, the first step to the coveted "wings." After two months, they moved on to a stint at Service Flying School, where they left the old biplanes behind: those who would become spitfire fighter pilots trained on single-engine planes; double-engine planes were assigned to those who would fly heavy, long-distance bombers — the Halifaxes, Stirlings and, eventually, the deadly Lancasters.

Wearing the airmen's badges and insignia earned in their six months of training, the Canadian airmen arrived in England, a country already visibly damaged by war. The much publicized month-long Battle of Britain was only the beginning of a devastating air siege that would last until May, 1941, and be inaccurately known as "The Blitz." Sometimes the Germans bombed ports and railway centres. Sometimes they released high explosives and incendiary bombs on the centre of cities. Sometimes they simply dropped bombs. With no clear idea of what they wanted to do and no pilots trained for night operations, their bombs had devastated not only the core of the City of London but also the East End and many provincial cities. By the end of the war, 3,500,000 houses would be destroyed and 30,000 British civilians would be killed by German bombs.

At night, when the air-raid sirens wailed, the homeless and

A flight of Lancasters on a bombing
mission to Germany.

Air force women in the operation room, Bomber Group.

the tens of thousands who could not afford bomb shelters crowded into the underground for protection. On furlough in London, nicknamed "The Big Smoke," the newly arrived Canadians saw people sleeping in wooden bunks along the side of the subway, families piled on the stairs and crowded on the concrete, side by side, to the edge of the tracks — "Night after night," remembers Brown. "For years on end," adds Harvey.

Brown and Harvey were bomber pilots, part of Bomber Command, the division of the RAF charged with bombing Germany. They would not be fighting German planes one-on-one in the sky over London. They would be flying large aircraft with heavy bombloads into Germany.

The Canadians arrived in Scotland aboard the old troopship, the *Queen Elizabeth*, and went on to the next leg of training. "We got onto a little old train like you see in the comics. All new and exciting," recalls Harvey. "Jumped on that and travelled seven hours all the way down through England to Bournemouth, on the south coast.

"This was the Canadian reception centre for people coming overseas. Got everybody sorted out. And while you waited to be funnelled as fighters or night fighters or bombers or whatever, you were drilled and marched every day. Keep yourself occupied.

"I guess it was six weeks we were there waiting. And then, geez, the big day finally comes and we were posted to an advanced flying unit, an AFU.

"And that was good because you got British instructors, RAF instructors. We often had a hard time from the RAF ground types, the CO [commanding officer] and administrative staff — but the flying staff was different.

"You could be a pilot with your wings but you hadn't done any serious flying. In Canada you weren't allowed to fly in cloud and whatnot. Not even night flying. No instruments, only total visibility. They were getting enough crashes without guys going out in the clouds.

"In England, of course, it was a different cup of tea. You were just never out of the clag. You were on the clocks constantly and those RAF guys were great at it. We couldn't understand them half the time, with their mouth full of marbles and a big rope of scarf around their necks. Funny looking guys, but Christ, they could fly. They taught us without any screaming or yelling like the Canadian instructors. Very quiet, very calm. Nothing rattled them. They never flapped about anything or panicked. And there was no

Ken Brown, 22, from Moose Jaw, Saskatchewan, in Bournemouth, England, 1942.

Canadian pilots inspect their
Lancasters at a Yorkshire
aerodrome.

apprehension at all. They just took it as if you were riding a
bicycle.

" 'Have you got wings?' they'd say.

" 'Yes, Sir.'

" 'Okay. That's an airplane. Go fly it. Here's the handbook.
Better read it to know where the tits and taps are, how much
gas and how to put the wheels down and whatnot. But it's an
airplane and you're a pilot; fly it.'

"They taught you to fly in foul weather with the utmost
confidence. Taught you to trust your instruments."

After the AFU, Canadian pilots and crew were sent to the
Operational Training Unit (OTU) where they lived in Nissen
huts — a kind of metal igloo made by arching sheets of iron
over a concrete pad. Inside the huts were 12 iron cots. Off-
duty hours were often spent huddled over the tiny coal stove
that failed to warm the damp Scottish winter. At OTU, they
honed their flying skills and practised dropping dummy bombs
filled with sand.

"Operational training was rough," Brown recalls. "There
was one night when five of us scheduled to fly a cross-country
came to the flight briefings convinced we shouldn't go up: it
was pouring rain, with a ceiling about 200 feet. And we
weren't flying the greatest aircraft in the world. We thought
the flight would be scrubbed but it wasn't.

"We took off and we had a 120-mile-an-hour wind at

10,000 feet, low for a wind of that size. Fortunately I put my battery radio-signal on and I turned back on course but the three fellows behind us just kept on flying and were lost out in the North Sea. The fourth fellow was lucky enough to land at an aerodrome in Scotland.

"When we landed, the winds were so strong that they had to tie us down exactly where we rolled to a stop. And believe me, we were very pleased to get down. But they seemed to take it so casual that, yes, they had lost three aircraft last night."

Over 8,000 air crew would die in training during the course of the war, including Eric Simonds, the brother of General Guy Simonds, who would command the 2nd Canadian Corps in Normandy. These deaths represented one seventh of all the casualties in Bomber Command.

"There were eight of us that started the course, and two of us that actually graduated. And the rumour was that if you could get through Kinross OTU, you could get through a tour of operations. We had hopes then."

It was at OTU that the pilots "crewed up." This gave the Brits from the old boys' network, chums from Oxbridge, Eton, Harrow and Rugby, the opportunity to find each other. But the Canadians didn't know that.

"They got you into a big room," recalls Harvey, "and all of a sudden you're seeing guys with navigator's badges, observer's badges, air gunners and whatnot; various operators. And they say, 'Okay, sort yourselves out. You've got to have crew.' And most of the people did it the only way you could. You didn't know the navigator or anything. Finally you find yourself talking to a guy and you look and he's got an observer's wing and he sees you've got your pilot's wings. And you're talking, conversing together, so you figure you're pretty compatible and that's what you need to be locked together in the cockpit for quite a while."

And what happened to the guys nobody wanted?

"All the jerks got on one airplane," says Harvey. "The jerk pilot and the jerk navigator: that's the only way it could possibly have worked."

For his Halifax, a four-engine bomber, Harvey chose a seven-man crew — a rear-gunner, a bomb-aimer, a navigator, a radio operator, a pilot, an engineer and a mid-upper gunner. "That was interesting because as well as flying together, you were sorting out personalities, on the side, over a beer. And kind of learning a little about each other. We had five Canadians and two English kids, initially."

Airmen of Squadron 423 hug after
surviving another mission.

When the time came for pilot Ken Brown to form a crew,
he hedged his bets.

"I did it the sneaky way. I went down to the Chief Ground
Instructor's office. He had a large board there with everyone's
name on it — bomb-aimers, navigators, gunners — and their
marks. And I took down the names of the guys who were at
the top of the list and asked every one of them. There was a
guy by the name of Sherry who was a 98 percenter. I asked him
first but he was crewed up with another Scot. So I asked
number two. And that was my navigator. And I did that all the
way down. I figured I needed the best if I was going to survive."

At OTU, while the men were getting to know each other,
they rehearsed for war.

"We did some fighter simulations where old Spitfires would
come running at you and you'd learn to corkscrew and the
gunners would give you commands to evade as if it was an
enemy fighter," Harvey reports. "And you'd do a lot of
bombing on the bombing range and you worked with the
gunner on that. 'Left, left, right, right, steady, steady, right,
steady, bomb's gone.' That routine. You got that drilled in your
head. The wireless operator was doing his thing. And the
navigator, on long cross-countries both day and night was
doing his job, plowing up and down across the landscape,
perfecting his 'dead-reckoning' — guiding the plane by
watching for lakes, villages, railway tracks and other landmarks
below."

"We always said that if you wanted a perfect crew, you'd have a Canadian pilot," says Moffat with a laugh. "He'd have common sense. You would have a British navigator because he had ice water running through his veins. And you would have two harebrained American gunners. The worst thing you could have was an Australian pilot because he was drunk most of the time."

Approximately nine months after they arrived in England, the Canadian recruits were declared "operational" and sent to join their squadrons: Harvey to 408, the "Goose" Squadron based in Leeming; Moffat, now a gunner, to 427, stationed at Topcliffe; Favreau to the Alouettes; Brown to the Coastal Command charged with keeping German ships off the North Atlantic.

YORKSHIRE

Most of the Canadians were scattered among the Royal Air Force bases established near the quiet villages of the Yorkshire Midlands, in the northeast corner of England.

The adolescents and young men Harvey described as "fresh and fuzzy-tailed" found themselves commanded mostly by British RAF and, as air crew, treated to British upper-class institutional perks.

"I have white sheets. I have a batman. I come from the squadron at night and I have to dress for dinner," says Moffat, whose grandparents were working-class Yorkshire folk. "I can't just slovenly go into the mess. My uniform is all neatly pressed, my shoes are shining, the socks are laid out, the shirts, the ties, everything is laid out on the side of my bed."

Every airman had a batman whose job it was to shine his shoes, clean his room, prepare tea and keep his wardrobe in shape. When the ever-increasing volume of commissioned air crew depleted the supply of male attendants, young women from the Women's Auxiliary Air Force took their place.

"One of her important duties was to awaken you each morning with a knock on the door," recalls Harvey, "and you were always asked, the night before, 'What time shall I knock you up in the morning, sir?' When the early morning knock came she would have a cup of tea in her hand. If you played possum, she'd be forced to open the door and give you a gentle shaking to arouse you. It always did."

Dubbed "the Brylcreem Boys" by their army counterparts,

Group exercises near a Yorkshire
Royal Air Force base.

Members of Squadron 403 let off
steam by chasing a flock of geese in
Kenley, England.

Canadian airmen show an English woman how to skate in Durham, England.

the air crew stationed in the countryside kept in close contact with civilian life. Unlike Flash Clayton, who could barely speak to a woman after three and a half years in Japanese POW camp, the men in Yorkshire talked to women every day.

"With so many men overseas, there were more English women in the pubs than men," says Harvey. "But an additional factor was the nightly air-raid duties that all civilian men performed. The wives of the volunteers would sit in the pubs and growl about the bloody war, the bloody Germans, and bloody Herbert, who was never home."

The Canadians helped gather the Yorkshire harvests and became regulars at pubs like the Shoulder of Mutton and the Black Swan, nicknamed the Mucky Duck.

"On nights when the weather was too bad for flying, the bomber men would come riding on their bicycles into our village of Sutton-on-the-Forest," recalls one Yorkshireman. "Some would go into the Black Swan pub but most would walk up and down the streets, talking to people, looking at the gardens and handing out gum to us kids. They were good to us. Not just the things they gave us, but the way they treated us — as if we were their kid brothers back home. They used to take away my father's Alsatian dog and get it drunk. Once they did the same thing to our goat."

Pumped up with adrenalin from the missions flown and those to come, the young air force men left footprints on the ceiling of the mess, raced their bikes across the floor and staggered into elephant fights:

"You'd get big leather chairs at each end of the room," says Moffat. "Everybody was canned by this time and you'd get four or five guys behind each chair. Commander Turnbull would be there at the light switch: 'Forty-seven, are you ready? Forty-nine, are you ready? Lights out. CHARGE!' ... across the hardwood floors in a mess about 75 feet long and 45 feet wide, coming from each direction, four or five guys pushing the chairs to crash in the centre."

As the evening progressed, the party broke into groups, some to play cards, some to shoot craps. Most clustered around the piano singing away what Doug Harvey called their "lonely, homesick, frightened, powerless" selves.

> That was a cute little rhyme,
> Sing us another one
> Just like the other one
> Sing us another one, do.
>
> There was a young plumber from Dee
> Who was plumbing his girl by the sea,
> Said the girl, stop your plumbing,
> For I hear someone coming,
> Said the plumber, still plumbing, it's me.
>
> There once was a man named Skinner,
> Who took a young girl out to dinner,
> At quarter to nine they sat down to dine,
> At quarter to ten it was in her.
> No, not the dinner, but Skinner.
>
> There was a young queer from Khartoum,
> Who took a young friend to his room,
> They argued all night, over who had the right
> To do what and with which to whom.
>
> That was a cute little rhyme,
> Sing us another one, do...

The airmen made the best of life in the air force, but from

Two Canadian flyers dressed for a mission. The airman on the right holds his "good luck" doll.

the beginning they were affronted by the prejudice dispensed by their British superiors along with the clean linen and afternoon tea. Harvey never forgot the words of the CO who briefed him on arrival:

"He was a real Brit, an RAF type. And he said things like, 'Now we know you're all like the red Indians, the savages, you Canadians, and we won't tolerate any of your antics over here.' We'd come to save the world, and this is what we got."

Before long the Canadians were pushing to do things differently than the Royal Air Force. Normally in the RAF, only the pilot was awarded a commission; the rest of the air crew were junior ranks. The Canadians petitioned to award a commission to all members of the air crew, in recognition of the rigorous training they had undergone and the deadly risk they volunteered to face.

"Nonsense," decided Air Vice Marshall Harris, known as Bomber Harris to the press and, before long, "Butcher" Harris to the airmen. "Many air crew have no officer qualities. The policy proposed by Canada would have the effect of depreciating the value of commissioned rank."

Unable to modify the British commissioning rules, the Canadian officers lobbied British High Command for more complete Canadianization of their squadrons. They didn't like the RAF siphoning off the most experienced new men to their

The brilliant mathematician, Freeman Dyson, was 19 when he joined the Operational Research Section of Bomber Command.

own units. After all, a quarter of the RAF was Canadian — more air crew were from Canada than from any other Commonwealth country.

First World War fighter pilot Gus Edwards led the campaign. "Our men in the RAF are being dispersed all over hell's half acre. We should never have participated with the British. We should have built an air force of our own."

Air Vice Marshall Harris sent the "sonofabitch Edwards" back to Canada.

But eventually, in early 1943, the British agreed to let the Canadians form their own bomber group within the RAF — No. 6 Bomber Group. It comprised 13 heavy-bomber squadrons. Every squadron had 15 aircraft with two full crews for alternate days. By the peak of the war, the 15,000 Canadians in No. 6 were living on six airfields near Allarton Hall, the commandeered British country house that acted as headquarters for Canadian wing commanders. Canadians named their squadrons to remind them of home — Goose, Thunderbird, Moose, Bison, Bluenose, Alouette. The Group's insignia reflected its dual allegiance — a maple leaf superimposed on the rose of York, the flower of their British home base.

Still, it was British commanders who decided where and when Canadians dropped their bombs. And in the press and on the radio, the Canadian airmen killed and wounded were still counted as RAF statistics. Even more galling, the Canadian squadrons were given particularly antiquated equipment.

According to Freeman Dyson, a brilliant 19-year-old mathematician attached to the Operational Research Section, the brain trust that gave scientific advice to Bomber Harris, "Six Group got the worst of everything. They got the worst equipment, the worst weather and usually the highest losses."

THE FLYING TRENCHES

For Moffat, Harvey, Favreau, Brown and the other Canadian air crew in the squadron, the task of bombing Germany settled into a tense routine.

Typically, the day started with a shake on the shoulder and the call, "You're on tonight."

You'd be trucked to the airfield at seven, and if you lived off-base you'd stay there until takeoff, after dark — overseeing repairs, checking the bomb bay, testing your aircraft.

All day long you'd be apprehensive, wondering, "Where to, tonight? Berlin again? The Ruhr? One of the hot spots? Where?"

"And we'd guess," says Harvey. "The shorter the target, the less gas, the more bombs. If you saw the refuellers putting the whole load on, 2,154 gallons, you knew it was a long stooge."

At four o'clock you'd gather in the briefing room. Every eye was on the red ribbon stretched across the large wall map of Continental Europe: tonight's flight path.

"Berlin. Christ," says Harvey. "You could just see the hearts sinking down through the boots, the faces getting a little wan. If it was another target, perhaps one you'd never been to before, like Hannover or Leipzig, you wouldn't really know how to react. But you knew about Berlin, even if you hadn't ever been there. That was the big one, the big city."

You'd listen as the Intelligence Officer traced the route — across the North Sea, across Holland, Belgium or France — to the German strike zone. You'd tune out as he circled the fighter bases along the way, pointing out where he expected you'd find searchlights, encounter flak.

"You knew damned well you were going to get into heavy searchlights," says Harvey. "You knew damned well you were going to get into heavy flak."

It was a relief when the meteorological expert stood up.

"We used to call that met guy Cloudy Joe. There was never any good news. And the poor guy didn't have the information that they have today. He didn't know what the hell was happening on the Continent. From the weather stations, he knew a bit about the fronts coming in, but predicting the weather in England is a crap shoot. And he would tell you all kinds of nonsense like the base would be open, and when you got back, of course, it was foggy. And the target would be clear tonight; no trouble finding it. And of course it was ten-tenths cloud. It was so ridiculous, it relieved the pressure a little bit for me.

"The other guy that relieved the pressure was the Canadian CO, who didn't fly on the operations. He was a peacetime RCAF type, about 35 years old, which was an old man to us young air crew guys. And he would be smoking his pipe — all the commanders had to puff a pipe — and all the old clichés would come out: 'Good hunting, God speed, we'll see you back here for briefing.' You know, he made it sound easy. Well, if it was that damned easy why wasn't he leading us?"

An analyst checking aerial
reconnaissance photos after a
mission.

You'd troop into the mess for supper. There'd be 25 or 30
men eating — or too nervous to eat. Nobody talked much.
You were on ops so you were in battle dress. And along with
the mutton, boiled potatoes and peas, you'd get an extra
poached egg.

From the mess hall, you'd funnel past the chaplain, the
rabbi, the priest. Maybe you'd give the padre a letter home to
Canada, just in case you didn't make it, or your girlfriend's
picture, for good luck.

You'd suit up in the locker room. The gunner would dress
for the Arctic. For six hours he sat in his turret in below-zero
temperatures, wind whistling through holes cut in the bubble
for better visibility. Gunners took longest to dress.

"The pilot had the Mae West, the chute harness, and his
boots and that's it," says Moffat. "And the navigator and the
bomb-aimer would put a jacket over top.

"We had the whole kit: the big flying boots, the electric
suit, the overall that zipped over, the jacket, the silk gloves,
the woollen gloves, the electric gloves over top. They snapped
on and we plugged them in. We had electric current in the

turret. I remember once going to Berlin and it short-circuited. I just about froze to death."

A few gunners put their girlfriends' silk stockings under their socks. Favreau stuffed his uniform with newspapers.

"Good insulation," he discovered. "*The Montreal Star* one leg. *La Presse* on the other. *La Presse* was best!"

You'd make a ritual of dressing, take your time about it. Moffat pinned a little rag doll, gift from a girl, on his battledress. He checked his wallet for the charm he always carried, "a piece of an officer's tie. During ground duty, there was a New Year's party and there's a tradition — you clip the officers' ties. I kept mine as a good luck charm."

You'd go to the trucks that take you to the airplane. Moffat's talisman was hidden under layers of dress, but at every boarding Moffat saw his navigator take out a stuffed toy lion and drag it along the ground, to the plane.

On some nights, as many as 1,000 Lancasters filled the sky as they took off for a bombing run to Germany.

You'd watch the setting sun pull the last light from the sky. The gunners peed on the tail wheel. You climbed into your own plane. Your baby. W-for-Willie was Moffat's baby. S-for-Sugar was Harvey's.

Then, the pilot revved the motors; the navigator examined his gauges; the aimer checked that the bombs were secure. You eyed the control tower — a white flare meant the mission was scrubbed. A green signal from the lantern meant go.

To avoid detection, you'd taxi and take off in strict radio silence. From neighbouring airfields, up to 1000 planes took to the air — "the stream" — directed to the same target.

With planes fully fuelled and loaded with bombs, the crews had a slim chance of surviving even a minor crash. And with so many planes taking off in succession in the dark, without radio traffic control, collisions were inevitable. "Everybody was nervous," says Moffat. "The most dangerous part of the whole trip, we figured, was takeoff. Once takeoff was over your battle was half-won."

Safely airborne, you'd fly out over the North Sea, steeling yourself for the next hurdle — the searchlights.

"They're standing up on the coast as you're coming across the North Sea to Holland, Belgium, France. There's a wall of these damned things. Right on the coast," recalls Harvey. "It didn't matter where your target was, Berlin or whatever, you had to get through the coastal defences: these things would stand up, maybe move a little bit. And the master beam, the bluish-white one with radar control, would search around and find the bomber. Then the others, slave beams manually controlled from the ground, would cluster around the bomber. Then the flak would hose at them. Or a fighter would come in."

Sometimes you got out of the searchlights and sometimes you didn't. Either way, it was terrifying.

"One of the beams would pick us up and the dark interior of the plane would burst into brightness like a star," says Favreau. "It was more devastating than being shot at. You had the feeling everyone was watching *you*. Every gunner, every fighter had picked *you* out. To get out we dived. We dived so hard my nose was bleeding, my ears were bleeding from the pressure."

Sometimes the planes flew ten minutes or more trapped in the cone of light. Secretly, you'd wish your best friend dead rather than land in one. "You were heartbroken to see a guy beside you coned," says Harvey. "But your mind said, 'Hold that bastard, hold it, till I get past ... Jesus, don't shoot him

Aircrew with the Porcupine Squadron awaits news of planes returning late from a mission.

down yet, I'm not past yet, I've got to sneak by here, in this dark space between these two great big cones.' "

Harvey remembers one night watching the beams scan the sky. Then, suddenly, he was coned. "You're blind. You can't see the hand in front of your face. You can't see any of your instruments. You can't see any of your controls. The gunners can't see anything either because the cockpit's a glass house and turrets are, too. You're deadly afraid they're coning you for a fighter. Fighters know you can't see out. You're in that spotlight. You're a sitting duck.

"You just ducked down in your seat, put the nose down and went hell for leather down. Couldn't see the air-speed indicator, of course. You're blinded. It's dark. And after that you begin to think how high you are. You can't see the ground or anything. So you start easing back because you figure it's not so great running into the ground. You might as well get shot down as do that."

If you made it through the searchlights and flak, you'd fly in absolute darkness.

"Blackness again, complete blackness," continues Harvey, "because there's no lights on the ground. None in the air you could see. And the navigator's working away, and the old

Pilot Frank Phripp (left), 26, from Newmarket, Ontario, and a friend between bombing missions.

engines are humming. You have no lights on in the airplane. You got fluorescent dials and your plotters and you're flying like that. And that would go on three hours maybe."

Pathfinders flew ahead dropping flares to identify the target. The bomb-aimer looked down — through a tiny window in the hull of the plane, through the darkness — to identify the bombing site.

Now you'd be the aggressor. You would release the bombs on the enemy target. You kept an eye out for the night-fighters — and for your own guys, too.

"On one operation, my plane and my friend Andy's were side by side heading for Germany," recalls pilot Frank Phripp. "Andy and I believed in speed over the target, so we would start high then do a dive. As we made this run there was no flak, no fighters, a piece of cake. But another Lanc, above Andy, let his bombs go. They went right through Andy's aircraft, and continued on down. Suddenly a flash of flame and smoke where Andy's aircraft had been — no parachutes."

If you bombed the target and the plane was okay, you'd head back to base, back through the blackness, the searchlights, low on fuel because you'd dodged a couple of German planes, exhausted, dreading the final ordeal of landing.

Then, just before dawn, as the skylarks started to sing, you'd head in, maybe remembering, as Brown would, a similar morning when a Lancaster — its navigator dead, the pilot badly wounded — got to the airfield and flipped on its back.

"The plane came apart. The turret rolled right across the airfield like a ball. The rest of the plane broke up. The rear-gunner was still in the turret, the guns embedded in his body. His legs were up around his ears. A mess, but he was alive. When he spoke, even though it was sort of garbled, I realized he was a Canadian. And he said, 'If you move anything I'll die.'

"So I said to him, 'Where are you from?'

"And he said, 'Ontario. It's good to be with a Canadian when I go.'"

Let's say you got down alive. You filed back into the ops room for debriefing. On the blackboards at the front of the room you saw the names of the crews out that night and their estimated time back. You saw Mary Dups, the English girl nicknamed Bubbles, write your name on the board. And you tried not to think of the empty spaces.

"You'd fill the names in as the time went on, because some

A Canadian airman from Squadron 617 is debriefed after a dam raid in Germany, May, 1943.

of the crews would come straggling in a bit late," says Dups. "Or you'd hear that someone had landed away at Trifield or somewhere like that. And then you could put another name in. You'd hope against hope that nobody would be missing, that they would all be back."

And then Dups would debrief you — with that sweet voice and those pinchable round cheeks. And so you'd try...

"They'd be tired and still joking a bit," says Dups. "They still managed to joke, you know. That was one of the wonderful things about Canada I didn't realize before — what a bunch of jokers they can be amongst themselves. And of course, this has an enormously enlivening effect if they are a bit down in the dumps. I think that's why they teased me such a lot."

You'd tell Bubbles what time the bombs went, what you'd seen in the sky and on the ground, the co-ordinates of the planes that went down off the coast. You'd joke, but as tired as you were, you'd be meticulous so whoever could, would be rescued as quickly as possible. And you knew Bubbles was thinking, "These poor devils," that she appreciated the no fussing around, that she cared. You knew you stank. And you weren't surprised when you heard your buddy say, "Gee, Bubbles, I love your scent. You don't smell like shit and fear."

Many young English women worked for Canadian squadrons.

THE FIRST MISSIONS

The saving grace for new recruits was the official RAF line that the better you were, the less chance you'd die. Whiz-kid

The Lancasters settled into a stream for the three- to four-hour flight to Germany.

Dyson's first study at Operational Research supported this contention, concluding that an airman's chances of surviving a mission increased with experience. Bomber Command brass were delighted.

Unlike the recruits sent into the Battle of Hong Kong, the airmen in No. 6 Group were incredibly well trained, but they had no experience. The first few times they left England and crossed the Channel to drop real bombs, they were taut with apprehension.

On his inaugural mission, Doug Harvey headed for the Ruhr

Canadians eventually mustered their own Bomber Group and painted their planes with symbols of home, like this "Ville de Quebec" emblem on the side of a 425 Alouette Squadron Lancaster.

in an old Halifax as co-pilot to the squadron leader. Before they could reach "Happy Valley," Harvey's plane was coned and hit.

"You don't hear any noise because your airplane is roaring. You can't even converse normally in the cockpit except over radio telephone, through earphones. So you couldn't hear the German night-fighters; you couldn't hear the bullets. You could see the tracers lashing around and you could sure hear the gunner shouting at the pilot to fire.

"The fighters knocked out the constant speed unit on the starboard engine. When it goes, the propeller just windmills, so we're on three engines. With the bombload we've got, we're starting to lose height. Can't hold 20,000 feet. Then two fighters shot at us and knocked out the other starboard engine. We manage to bomb the target but we're losing height rapidly. The pilot orders the gunner to throw out the guns, dump anything loose over the side to lighten the airplane. We're struggling to get back to the Channel — so we can ditch. And it is questionable whether we were going to make it.

"I suggested that we start up that starboard engine. There was a great pause. I'm a sergeant. He's a squadron leader. He's the captain. It's my first trip. It's his 13th. So anyway he started it up and we were up to three engines so we sailed off and landed in the south of England."

Takeoff became increasingly hazardous as Bomber Command kept upping the bombload.

"You start building the speed, slowly, slowly, like a great lumbering truck," says Harvey. "And then, with the stick forward as far as you can get it, you try to get that tail up. Finally, 60 miles an hour, 70, and you watch the end of the runway and the trees just off it, everything alert, and then finally, 80, 85, 90, the engineer pushing the throttles so they won't slip back. Finally 100 and you've started easing back, because you don't want to jerk it off in case you stall — lose an engine, you're gone.

"So you just work it up slowly, watching the trees. Sometimes so heavily loaded, you're just skimming them. It's dark, but you know damn well how close you are. Milking this thing up very gingerly — 120, 125 — the engineer snapping up the wheels as soon as you give him the word. 'Wheels up.' And then finally you got flying speed and you start to climb. And the sweat's dripping down. Get up you bastard. Yeah. Yeah."

Harvey remembers the night he and his crew were taxiing down the runway at 100 miles an hour for what should have been a routine ascent. But the control column jammed. With the help of his engineer, he managed to get the plane off the ground before it hit the trees.

"It was vibrating all over the place. We started checking things, yelling at the crew to check the control rods that run back through the fuselage, check the automatic pilot. We're busy wrestling with the plane because with this big bombload on it, it wants to turn over, and we're trying to nurse it up to enough height so we can all bail out.

"We got it milked up to 5,000 feet and I told the crew to prepare to abandon ship. I kept calling each position to make sure they'd all gone — 'bomb-aimer, navigator, wireless op, engineer...' Before Harry, the engineer, went, I said, 'Give me my chute.' So Harry clipped it onto my hooks but instead of

In May, 1942, Bomber Harris sent 1,000 bombers to destroy Cologne, Germany. Bridges and buildings crumbled, but within two weeks, the city was back to normal.

clipping it on so the parachute handle was on the right, he put it on me so the handle was on the left.

"Then Harry goes and I am all alone. Steve, the bomb-aimer, has left the trap door open and the air is just smashing, blasting up through there.

"So the airplane's trying to roll over and I'm desperately holding on to it and trying to get out of the seat. And coming by these four throttles, the rip cord caught on the knobs and popped the chute right in the aisle. So I'm standing there with this white parachute all over me saying to myself, 'Oh shit. You've had it now.'

"Anyway, I was clawing the chute off the throttles, the airplane's rolling over and going down — with the bombload

Unaware that German civilians were the secret target of their missions, Canadian air crew proudly recorded successful strikes on the noses of their planes.

— and I'm pulling the chute off my head so I can try and find my way out in the dark. I'm saying to myself, 'Well, it's better to get out than stay in here.' The aircraft's on its back and I just manage to dive through the hole in the nose. The chute comes, too.

"The plane went down and blew up a farmer's barn; killed the farmer, poor fellow. He was 90 years old and he heard our airplane coming down and he'd come running out to see what had happened and unfortunately he got blown up with the aircraft."

Doug Harvey experienced the terror of a bomber raid from the pilot's cockpit. The tail gunner, crouched in his plastic bubble, cut off from the rest of the crew by metal doors, saw the operation from the plane's rear.

"The coldest spot in the aircraft was the rear turret," says Brown. "Poor old gunner, sitting there in 50 degrees below zero. And unfortunately my gunner often breathed through his mouth. The oxygen mask would freeze right onto his face. I'd call him on the intercom and say, 'Mack, Mack,' just to get an answer from him. Then when he didn't answer, I knew he had passed out.

"So I'd say to the radio operator, 'Huey, go down and get Mack. He's passed out again.' Down he would go. Come back up and say, 'Skip, he's breathing again.' Lo and behold, half an hour later, Mack would be out cold again — no oxygen, pass out. So go back again through the same sequence. Some trips, he was out six times."

On Jim Moffat's third mission — a bombing run over Mannheim — the plane was hit by a German night-fighter. The tail gunner and wireless operator were killed, the engineer wounded. Moffat was manning the mid-upper guns.

"On this trip, we found out what it was all about. The bullets went through the bomb-hold. These bombs were full of oil and phosphorus which starts pouring out and catches fire. It's just like a big blowtorch. So I said, 'Skipper, we got bags of fire out here.' And he said, 'I can see it.' So he dove, put the plane in a steep dive and lost two or three thousand feet, put the fire out.

"We aborted the mission and headed for home. All hydraulics were gone. We couldn't get the wheels down, couldn't open the bomb doors. We still had our bombload.

"When we made it to our own 'drome they said, 'Aim it out to sea and everybody bail out.' But the skipper said, 'Well, no I can't. I've got wounded on board. If we push him out he may not be found and may bleed to death.'

"So they said, 'Well, give us a half hour to get everybody in the air-raid shelters.'

"So they sound the siren and we're flying around in circles, and the engineer has passed out. He comes to and says, 'Where are you?' And we tell him we're circling so we can belly-land. And he says, 'Oh, you can get the wheels down.' And we say, 'There is no hydraulics.' And he says, 'All we have to do is cut the hydraulic pipe and they'll fall down by themselves.' So we drag him over to it, and he's trying to show us but he passes out.

"We fly around some more. He comes to three different times and he finally tells us which one to cut. We cut the pipe, the wheels come down, the green lights come on, we land. And as soon as we stop, the plane bursts into flames again. So they douse us with foam and they say, 'Where is your cookie, the big bomb, the 2,000-pounder?'

"So they dashed down to the end of the runway. No bomb.

We found out later that a 20-millimetre cannon hit us and cut the steel cable that holds the bomb under the plane. The bomb must have fallen through the bomb doors.

"That night they put the aircraft in a hangar and locked the hangar. It was the first time anyone had come back with wounded and a badly shot-up aircraft. Usually when you get hit, everybody bails out, the plane crashes. They didn't want anybody to see it. It would be too demoralizing."

To buoy up his spirits, Moffat went into Harrogate, to the tavern that used to be an old theatre. He had a few pints, went up on the stage and sang his heart out. "Ol' Man River" was his favourite.

> You and me,
> We sweat and strain,
> Body all achin' and
> Racked with pain.
> Tote that barge!
> Lift that bale!
> Get a little drunk
> And you land in jail.
>
> I get weary
> And sick of tryin',
> I'm tired of livin'
> And scared of dyin';
> But ol' man river,
> He just keeps rollin' along!

Moffat loved to sing. He and his friend, Red Soeder, finished their drunk and staggered to the rooms they'd rented nearby. "I had my mind made up," he later said. "My grandfather died in the Boer War, my father barely survived the First World War, and I figured I wasn't going to survive the Second World War. So I thought, 'Why should I worry? I'm not going to make it anyways, so I'll just have a good time as I go through.' That helped."

THE UNMANLY TRUTH

The life of the airmen was a manic swing between killing by night and an almost normal existence by day. For 40 hours a month, they feared for their lives. For the rest, they were "The Brylcreem Boys," safely ensconced on British soil.

They may have been the envy of the foot soldiers in the trenches, but this schizophrenic ricochet from battlefield to barracks took its own particular toll.

"It was like going to hell and coming back to paradise: Picadilly Circus, warm pubs, good times. Then the next morning back to hell," says Favreau. "This for me was the worst part, the to and fro. Many times, coming back from a raid, all by myself in the back of the airplane, I cried, I cried like a baby. I had to. That was the only way to get out of it."

The searchlights, the flak, the fighters, the bomb-weighted takeoffs, the mad race against the fuel gauge for home — each man had his own personal definition of hell. It would eat away at him. Some drank too much. Others developed an "operational stare" — that blank look that blocked out bad times and good times both. You'd see them alone in the pub, glass untouched, or in the locker room, boot in hand, focused on an invisible inner demon.

"Something had happened to them, a very bad incident — maybe a wreck, a crash. They lost their confidence," explains Harvey. "People can only stand so much stress. Their nerves just went."

They cracked.

"My rear-gunner, Ray, curly-haired, 19, normally full of humour, started screaming he was going to die," says Harvey. "It was unnerving the entire crew so I told the navigator to take the fire extinguisher. 'Hit the bastard over the head.'

"A minute later the screaming stops, and the navigator radioes me and says, 'He's gone.'

"I say, 'What do you mean he's gone?'

"Says the navigator, 'He jumped.'"

Some men simply refused to fly. They were brought before the Special Cases Committee. Nine officers decided how to label the charge: Inefficiency. Misconduct. Medical. Or LMF — Lack of Moral Fibre. In an unpublished manuscript, Harvey describes the degrading process of LMF:

"When an air crew member had gone to the limits of his courage and had, after much internal agonizing, forced himself to tell his commanding officer, 'I will not fly again. I will not fly no matter what you do to me,' he was immediately confined and separated from his crew and squadron members. He disappeared from their lives forever.

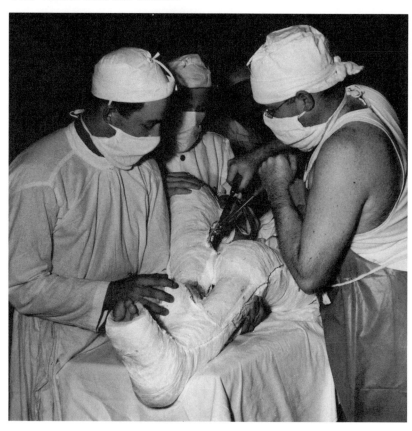

Canadian medics operate on an
airman wounded in a bombing raid.

There were no farewells, no explanations.

"The horror for the individual charged with LMF did not
diminish with his sentence. It ate silently at his insides like a
cancer and did not fade as the war years receded."

By the end of the Second World War, 4,000 Commonwealth
airmen would no longer be able to face their missions. They
were brought up on LMF charges. And, like "Ron Witts" at
North Killingholme Station, 627 Canadians were stripped of
their rank and publicly humiliated. One young man, paraded
as LMF, went behind a hangar and hanged himself.

"It was a horrible system," concludes Harvey. "These were
your crew mates and your buddies, branded cowards when you
knew they weren't. You never saw them again. 'Get them away
from the crew. Get them off the station. Or they'll infect all
the other air crew.' This was Bomber Harris' policy, of course."

Most of the airmen who faced their fears night after night in
the skies over Germany, put their faith in statistics. A tour of
duty was 30 missions and they had to complete at least 2 tours
of duty with only a short furlough between. Some volunteered

for a third. The most frightening part was the first 5 to 10 missions. Complete those, was the hope, and you would gain the experience that would bring you back alive. For some, the closer they came to the end of their tour, the cockier they got.

"My friend, Van de Kirkoff, he had a motorbike," says Moffat, "and we'd turn the lights out on a moonlit night and go 90 miles an hour up the highway, drink all night, then come zipping back. He went 29 ops, and I remember as though it were yesterday, he said, 'I've never had a fighter attack, I've never had flak, I've never been coned in searchlights... I think some of you guys are telling stories.' Of course, the thirtieth one, he never came back."

The chilling truth was that experience had little to do with the survival rate. When mathematician Freeman Dyson repeated his first study using fresh data, he drew new conclusions. "The total effect of all the skill and dedication of the experienced crews was statistically undetectable. Experienced and inexperienced were mown down as impartially as the boys who walked into the German machine-gun nests at the Battle of the Somme in 1916."

By the spring of 1943, the Canadians who huddled in the cockpits and turrets of their Halifax and Lancaster bombers knew that the chances of outliving the war were slim. They had seen the empty places in the mess hall. Too often, they had drunk to the toast,

Fill your glasses full, boys
Fill your glasses high
Here's to the dead already
And here's to the next to die.

Everyone had suffered more than enough harrowing experiences to last a lifetime.

But Hitler was running the world and they were going to stop him. Their risk was part of the price to be paid for disarming the enemy. And that was what they were doing, wasn't it? Blasting Hitler's military machine to bits?

If they had been told the true intent of their missions, the Boys in Blue might not have dropped their bombs so blithely.

The air war had started in 1940 with the Germans bombing imprecise targets. They then bombed the airfields in Kent. On one of the airfield raids, a German plane released a bomb over

London by mistake. The next day the RAF retaliated and bombed Berlin. The Germans bombed London.

And so began the "indiscriminate" bombing of cities that would continue throughout the war.

In 1940, Prime Minister Winston Churchill issued a secret memorandum to his Chiefs of Staff, ordering "an absolutely devastating, exterminating attack by very heavy bombers upon the Nazi homeland."

The same year, at the Berlin Sports Palace, Führer Adolph Hitler shrieked, "We will raze their cities to the ground. One of us will break, and it will not be National Socialist Germany."

In late 1942, Churchill appointed Arthur Harris Air Vice Marshall, head of Bomber Command, and charged him with carrying out the government's threat. Like the prime minister, Harris was convinced the air force could win the war; American Air Force commanders agreed. But army chiefs argued that, ultimately, only great land battles would defeat the Nazis, and so, they began preparations for an invasion of Normandy. Until the spring of 1944, these two strategies would wage war side by side, each convinced of its own logic.

Lacking in-flight radar, the British and Canadian bombers could only "precision" bomb in daylight. But without long-range fighter escorts to protect them during day missions, they raided by night, dropping explosives from high altitudes on industrial areas, hoping to hit something — anything — of importance. This was "indiscriminate" or "area" bombing. If they missed, well, they'd make a mess and at least destroy German morale.

In a secret memo, October, 1942, Air Marshall Sir Charles Portal framed Bomber Command's new policy: "I suppose it is clear that the new aiming points are to be the built-up areas, not for instance, the dockyards or aircraft factories."

In a meeting with the Chiefs of Staff Committee, Air Vice Marshall Harris enunciated his boss's policy: "We shall destroy Germany's will to fight. Now that we have the planes and crews, in 1943 and 1944 we shall drop one and a quarter million tons of bombs, render 25 million Germans homeless, kill 900,000 and seriously injure one million."

The heyday of "area" bombing would be 1943. The bombers pounded Germany with 48,000 tons of explosives in 1942, and with another 207,600 tons in 1943. Night attacks escalated, targeting Germany's most populous regions: the Ruhr, March to June, 1943; Hamburg, July to November, 1943; Berlin,

November, 1943 to March, 1944.

John Terraine, a historian sympathetic to the RAF, described Bomber Command's new secret policy "as a prescription for a massacre, nothing more, nor less." Yet the Canadians were told nothing.

BOMBING THE DAM

To win the war, the British aimed first to destroy the Ruhr Valley, Germany's industrial heartland. From March to June, 1943, British and Canadian air crew, including Harvey, Brown and Moffat, flew repeatedly over the Ruhr River Valley, heavily bombing its major cities — Dortmund, Duisburg, Gelsenkirchen. But the Germans seemed to rebuild their cities as soon as they were destroyed. Something else was needed.

In the green, rolling countryside, across rivers emptying into the Ruhr, a tributary of the Rhine, the Germans had built a series of dams. The dams irrigated the crops that fed the highly concentrated working-class population. More significant for the British military, the dams controlled the water level for an intricate network of canals crucial to barge transport, and powered the great steel plants and munitions factories of the German war machine.

Across the Channel in England, in a tranquil setting of hollyhocks, lavender and lobelia, Barnes Wallis, an eccentric British scientist, skipped stones in his garden pond. He would live to regret it, but for the moment he was using his spare time to perfect an irresistible bouncing bomb. The very something that was needed.

Ken Brown knew nothing of this. His night raid over Berlin at the end of February, 1943, was his 23rd mission: he had flown 15 operations in Coastal Command and another 9 with 44 Squadron. On March 1st, his entire crew was summarily transferred to Squadron 617.

"There was a hastiness about it," recalls Brown, "trying to get us loaded on the train and rolling. We heard all kinds of rumours. Nobody was telling you anything."

Except that the commanding officer had told Brown that he'd be "the backbone of the squadron. They need your experience." At the train station in Scampton, the 21-year-old pilot did a double-take. His new colleagues sported an impressive display of citations — Distinguished Flying Crosses, Distinguished Flying Medals, even a few Distinguished Service

A Lancaster from Squadron 617 drops the "bouncing" bomb, designed to breach the Ruhr Valley dams.

Orders. This was no ordinary squadron.

And the training itself was bizarre. Normally, pilots were reprimanded for flying too low; the Lancasters were designed to bomb from 20,000 feet and up. Five hundred feet was considered low-level flying.

Squadron 617 started at 250 feet and...

"When we got used to it, we went down to 150 feet. This was really low. But then they asked us to start flying at 60 feet, at night — this was a whole new experience. It was frightening. You had trees; you had high tension wires; many different obstacles. At that altitude, you can't be sloppy. If you dropped a wing at 60 feet, it'd scrape on the ground."

The airmen still knew nothing about Squadron 617 except that it seemed to include every hot-shot crew in England. It didn't even have the planes it would use for the actual operation. They borrowed a few and practised low-level flying with dummy bombs approximating the load they would carry. A few days before the raids, they got their planes and for the first time saw Barnes Wallis' top-secret bomb.

After two and a half months of training, Brown and the other air crew finally found out what they were supposed to destroy with the new bomb.

"Most of us thought it would be ships. Believe me, we were all really shocked when our commander told us we were going to do the dams, 'the great dams of Germany,' he said."

Now the men knew what their targets would be — the Lister, the Mohne, the Eder and the Sorpe, the largest dam of the Ruhr and the hardest to hit. They were told the size of the dams, the water they contained, the way the bomb would skip across the water, sink down beside the dam and explode to crack it open, the acres of German land their mission would flood. It took five tons of water for each ton of steel produced, they were told. If they were successful, the forces of nature would wreak more havoc than a thousand bombs, at less cost to the air force. It would have a tremendous impact on the war effort.

The "Dambuster Raid" was a public relations triumph. King George VI personally congratulates pilot Ken Brown, one of the lucky 50 percent of the flyers who came back from the raid alive.

"We were impressed — and frightened about the whole thing," says Brown. "We thought, 'Holy Moses, surely those dams are defended.' They showed us the booms strung across the face of the dam to defend it. You couldn't hit the boom — the bouncing bomb had to go over the boom and into the dam.

"The bomb had to be dropped exactly 60 feet at an exact air speed. As it struck the water, it spun backwards, pushing water up in front of it like a geyser. The first crew to try it had their tail snapped off by the column of spray and barely limped back to land.

"If you got over there without running into high tension wires, or someone filling your ass with lead, you were gonna be lucky. If you dropped the bomb, which most hadn't done yet, and got away with it, you were gonna be double lucky. And if you made it back, by God, you were gonna be lucky.

"I thought our possibilities were very slim indeed. It was a one-way ticket to the dams."

Brown and the other pilots filed back to their quarters, grim-faced. They couldn't even speak of their fear because they were sworn to silence until the other crews were briefed the next day. Brown wrote a "last" letter to his girlfriend. Many other men did the same, writing to mothers, fathers, wives and lovers. By the time the letters reached Canada, they thought, they would probably be dead.

A day after the briefing, on a clear night with a rising moon, 17 Lancaster bombers took off from the airbase at Scampton, headed for the dams in the Ruhr. Under each

Canadian air crew lost during the Dambuster Raid.

Vernon W. Byers (pilot)

Joseph G. Brady (rear gunner)

Alden P. Cottam (wireless operator)

A. Albert Garshowitz (wireless operator)

Vincent S. MacCausland (bomb aimer)

James McDonell (rear gunner)

Frank A. Garbas (front gunner)

James L. Arthur (bomb aimer)

Kenneth Earnshaw (navigator)

Floyd A. Wile (navigator)

Harvey S. Glinz (front gunner)

bomber was a massive bomb, so heavy that the planes barely cleared the hedge at the end of the runway. Brown's target was the Sorpe, over six hours from base. The crew flew low all the way into a valley socked in with fog. When he reached the dam — 125 feet of concrete, reinforced with a thick berm of earth wide enough to drive a truck across — Brown dove towards the water, narrowly missing the church steeple of the hillside village.

Again and again, Brown and his crew dove towards the dam, trying to fly low enough and at the prescribed trajectory to release the bomb. The other dams would be attacked with the bouncing bomb but because the Sorpe was so thick, Brown had to hit the dam directly on its face, near the top. Theoretically, the explosion would disperse the earth and crack the concrete. The force of the rushing water would finish the job.

On the eighth try, Brown got it right. The aimer released the bomb.

"When the damn thing went off, it was almost like the atomic bomb. It blew up all that water into a huge mushroom of rain."

Mission accomplished, Brown and his crew turned around. And, as Brown reports, "We went back along the Rhine and we had a bunch of incendiaries so we were dropping incendiaries on barges all the way down the Rhine. And we shot up a few planes. We were out to raise all the hell we could."

When Brown reached the Dutch coast, it was daylight and the flak guns on the Zaider Zee were waiting for him. At 5:30 a.m., after more than seven hours in the air, he returned to base. His plane was damaged by flak. One man was dead; two badly wounded. Brown would consider his crew lucky. Of the 17 aircraft that took off on the dam raid the night before, 8 returned. Brown was the only Canadian pilot to survive.

"When we came back from the dam raid, we discovered how many we had lost; good friends we knew. We'd seen some go down on the way in, blowing up in the air but we had no idea of the numbers until we got on the ground. And then it started to sink in."

Bomber Command was not in mourning; it was elated. Even though so many had died and the Sorpe had survived the bomb, two dams had been breached.

The raid was a resounding public relations success. King George awarded British Squadron Leader Guy Gibson the

Victoria Cross. Brown would be given the Conspicuous Gallantry medal. Huge headlines hailed the "perfect bombing," calling the operation a "decisive blow." Reports described the "two mighty walls of water" which had devastated the areas surrounding the dams. First reports claimed 10,000 Germans drowned. Industry was said to be out of commission, navigation on the Ruhr stalled. "A titanic blow at Germany." The "Dambusters' raid" seemed to justify the British strategy of "smart" bombing.

In the euphoria that followed, the unusually high losses were forgotten. Over 50 percent of the flyers never returned; 53 men died, 13 of them Canadians.

According to Brown, Barnes Wallis, the eccentric scientist who devised the bouncing bomb in his back garden, "wept. 'All those boys. All those boys,' he said."

Quickly, the Germans repaired the damaged dams. Steel production in the Ruhr valley doubled that year. Few remembered, or knew, that almost 1,300 people died in the floods following the dam bombing, many of them Ukrainian women and children, trapped in a German prisoner of war camp below the Mohne dam.

FIREBOMBING HAMBURG

At the end of July, 1943, in the tinderbox of a summer heat wave, Bomber Harris ordered his air force to begin a massive air raid on Hamburg, Germany's most important industrial centre and the largest seaport on the European Continent.

To protect the flyers, Bomber Command had a new technological trick, nicknamed "window." One of the crew would hurl thin strips of aluminum foil out the rear doors of the plane as it flew across German territory. Fluttering in the slipstream, the metal confused the radar that controlled the searchlights and flak guns, sending them swinging erratically across the sky. The Germans would eventually discover the ruse, but not before Hamburg was levelled during a week of devastating raids.

At 9 p.m., July 24, sirens wailed through the streets of Hamburg. People hurried to their basements and to the underground bunkers as bombs exploded a few miles away. Searchlights raked the sky. The people knew what they had to do. There was no particular panic.

Within minutes, high explosive, incendiary, phosphorus

During nine days in July, 1943,
Bomber Command air crew
dropped 9,000 tons of bombs on
the city of Hamburg, levelling it.

The firebombing of Hamburg
gutted 60 percent of the city and
killed 40,000 people.

and napalm bombs pounded the city core. Buildings erupted in flames that shot 20 feet into the sky. With hurricane force, 150 mile-per-hour winds were sucked into the oxygen vacuum created by the fire, ripping trees out by their roots, collapsing buildings, pulling children out of their mothers' arms. Twenty square miles of the city centre burned in an inferno that would rage for nine full days.

"There was no smoke, only flames and flying sparks like a snowstorm," recalls a German firefighter. "The heat melted the lens in my protective glasses. I saw a crowd of people lying and sitting on the street, moaning. They had given up. I joined them and lay down, put my steel helmet against the wind, and tried to suck oxygen from the pavement. My clothes kept catching fire and I had to beat the flames out. The air was so hot it burned my windpipe. Everyone around me died. The clothing on the women was baked off them, leaving their bodies naked. The bodies didn't burn but dried out completely."

The temperature in the firestorm reached 1,000 degrees Fahrenheit. There was no oxygen to breathe; whatever was flammable burst spontaneously into flame.

Inge Einspenner, 16 years old, was with her cousin in Hamburg, planning to join her parents at their cottage on the Ost See the next day.

"We were caught in a big, big fire," she recalls in halting English. "We came to a street crossing and the houses were all coming down on us. We didn't know where to go. Bombs were everywhere... We went this way, this way... We were lost. We were trying to go away from Hamburg.

"We went down in a basement of a house. Then the next minute, we heard a big bomb. So we went out of the house, on the street. And there was a large fire — all the houses.

"Everything was burning, even the paving stones in the street. We were blind from the fire. Burning dust. Ashes. People were burning. We went anywhere. We were only concerned to escape the fire.

"I saw a child stick in the tar in the street. And it didn't come out again. It burned to death. And the mother tried to save her child. But she couldn't. She made one step. That was all.

"A lady was seeing the girl burning and the mother sticking. Then she started to burn on her back, so she jumped into the river. But when she came out, she burnt again."

On August 2, 1943, Doug Harvey boarded his Halifax to fly the last of the four raids that firebombed Hamburg. It was his seventh mission; he had logged 500 hours and he felt as he always did when he flew over Germany — "in total terror that the German fighters were going to shoot me down."

Taking off over the North Sea, the plane headed into a solid bank of clouds. Even though the ground crew had rubbed anti-icing paste on the leading edges of the wings and sprayed the windscreen and propellers with de-icer, the Halifax was coated with a heavy, transparent shell. So thick was the cloud cover that Harvey didn't notice the ice. He was having a hard time controlling the plane. Thunderstorms erupted and lightning streaked the clouds.

"St. Elmo's Fire danced across the inside of the windscreen and all over the flying panel," says Harvey, "making it difficult to concentrate on the instruments."

In the distance, the clouds above Hamburg glowed red from the raging fires. A huge cumulus nimbus drifted into the flight path of the Halifax.

"If I got into that thunderhead our bomber would be in terrible danger. Trying to keep on course and yet avoid the storm, I inched my way around the storm cloud, or so I thought."

Without warning, the plane nosed into the cloud, stalled, and started a 15,000-foot spin. Harvey ordered the crew to bail out.

"The navigator, Eric, is yelling, 'Drop the bombs, drop the bombs!' So I yanked the bomb doors open and pulled the jettison handle and *pfft*, out went the bombs. We hadn't bombed the target. We had dropped it ten miles short."

The sudden opening of the huge bomb bay doors acted as an air brake and the Halifax slowly straightened into a dive. At 5,000 feet — after the 15,000-foot spin — Harvey got control of the plane. The force of gravity created by the wild plunge had pinned the crew members to their seats. "We were still there, most of us," says Harvey.

All but the wireless operator, Ray, who, en route to Hamburg, had suddenly screamed in terror, "Turn back, Skipper, turn back! We're all going to be killed! Please, Skipper, turn back!"

Ray jumped out the rear door of the aircraft, into the fire-reddened night sky, in the wake of the fluttering, metal strips.

There were four firebomb raids over Hamburg in nine days.

Except for the smouldering ruins and the fresh fires started by the succession of British and Canadian bombers, the city of Hamburg was black. There was no electricity. No water. Everything was wreckage and dead bodies. People were crushed under tons of bricks. Others were baked. Those who sought shelter in the underground bunkers suffocated. Families were asphyxiated in their cars.

In the summer heat, the bodies rotted and stank.

Rats and flies multiplied. Forty thousand people were dead. And the survivors, such as Inge Einspenner, would live forever with the horror and the incalculable loss.

Most of the dead were plowed into a mass grave dug in the shape of a cross. Timbers were erected, listing not individuals but entire city neighbourhoods. By the time the fires of Hamburg were put out, over 60 percent of the city had been destroyed. Almost a million people were homeless.

From the British military perspective, the Bomber Command incendiary attack on Hamburg was outstandingly successful. Only 9,000 tons of bombs had killed 40,000 people and reduced a major industrial port to ashes. "None of our other attacks had produced effects that were a tenth as destructive as the effects of a firestorm," wrote Dyson after the war. The operation was nicknamed "Gomorrah."

But bombers could only produce a firestorm when their planes were able to bomb without serious interference. Soon after Hamburg, the Germans developed radar to see through the Allies' aluminum-strip "windows." Only once more — Dresden, February, 1945 — would the British in the Second World War succeed in burning a city to the ground. Immortalized in Kurt Vonnegut's *Slaughterhouse Five*, justly subtitled "The Children's Crusade," the Dresden firebombing was the last time in the war that boys of 18, 19, and 20 were sent to pulverize cities that had stood for centuries.

Air Vice Marshall Harris was pleased with the Hamburg raids. To the outraged voices protesting the high civilian casualties, he replied, "In spite of all that happened at Hamburg, bombing proved a relatively humane method ... there is no proof that most casualties were women and children."

In fact, according to meticulous German records revealed later, of the 40,000 people killed, 20 percent were children. For every 100 men who died, 160 women were killed. In all, the body count was 13,000 men, 21,000 women and over 8,000 kids.

BOMBING THE NAZI HOMELAND

In that bloody, relentless winter of 1943-44, Bomber Command set its sights on Berlin, Germany's capital and Hitler's stronghold. In fulfillment of his slogan, "Victory Through Air Power," Harris vowed to devastate Berlin as completely as Hamburg: "We are going to produce in Germany by the first of April, 1944, a state of devastation in which surrender is inevitable."

Beginning in November, 1943, there would be 16 major raids on Berlin. On one February night alone, 1,000 Lancasters released 2,500 tons of explosives on the city. By the end of March, 1944, 50,000 tons of bombs would hit Berlin.

The airmen called Berlin "The Holy City": it was the most heavily defended target in Germany, over 2,000 direct air miles from the British bases, at the limit of the Lancaster's reach. To get there, the planes had to fly even farther, detouring hundreds of miles to avoid German anti-aircraft defences.

To save weight and thus increase the fuel and bombloads, Air Vice Marshall Harris wanted to strip back the defences of the planes, remove some of the protective armour and reduce the gunners' ammunition.

Freeman Dyson suggested another way to save weight: rip out the aerodynamically awkward turrets and eliminate the mid-upper and tail gunners from the crew, along with their heavy weapons. According to statistics, Dyson said, gunners could not defend the bombers against night-fighters, which most often attacked from the gunner's blind spot, below the plane.

"Privately, I had another reason for wanting to rip out the turrets," writes Dyson. "Even if the change did not result in saving a single bomber, it would at least save the lives of the gunners."

But to remove the gun turrets flew in the face of the romantic image of the gunner riding shotgun for his crewmates. The armour went; the ammunition was cut back; the turrets and gunners stayed.

The airmen assigned to the Berlin raids watched their friends disappear one by one. New crews arrived, were sent out and went missing before anyone got to know them: names were chalked up on the order-of-battle board, erased and replaced the next day. In the first three months of 1944, Harvey's squadron lost 20 crews.

The aim of the bombing was ostensibly to destroy the German military, yet, three-quarters of the Hamburg deaths were women and children.

"When I look back on those casualty figures today it seems incredible that I survived," says Harvey, "but at the time, I never measured the odds. Such faith belongs to the young and without it, I suppose, few would have flown. Viewed today it smacks of arrogance, conceit and stupidity. I can only admit that as I flew more and more raids, I grew more and more contemptuous of the dangers."

It was a good thing that Harvey was young.

And a good thing Jim Moffat was resigned to death.

In August, 1943, having finished gunnery school, Moffat joined a squadron that had just firebombed Hamburg. In their first few raids on Berlin, their plane was coned twice and was hit with flak that left 300 holes in the fuselage. But Moffat

Just back from a raid, these exhausted airmen have once again beaten the odds. Of the 125,000 air crew in Bomber Command, more than half were wounded or killed. They didn't know it, but experience had nothing to do with coming back alive.

survived. In an accident of fate, he was moved from the mid-upper turret to the tail gun. On the next trip, his replacement was killed by bullets from a German night-fighter.

The tail turret was a tight and dangerous fit for the lanky Moffat. His long legs cramped into position, making unfolding and bailing out of the rear turret next to impossible. In an emergency, he planned instead to push open the doors to the belly of the plane and crawl to the escape hatch in the middle. Normally, the tail gunner's parachute hung on a wall near the doors. To save time, Moffat wore the chute whenever he was in the air. If worst came to worst, he would jump to safety.

Officially, the word was that airmen had an excellent chance of survival if the plane were shot down. They would simply jump through the escape hatch, pull the rip cord on their parachutes and float down to earth.

The facts suggested otherwise: 50 percent of crew shot down in an American bomber escaped; from the older types of British night bombers such as the Halifax and the Stirling, 25 percent escaped; from the Lancaster, 15 percent.

At the time of the Berlin raids, Bomber Command was rapidly phasing out the old bombers and converting the squadrons to Lancasters, which had escape hatches only 22 inches wide — 2 inches narrower than in the Halifax. According to statistician Dyson, "The missing 2 inches probably cost the lives of several thousand boys."

"Indiscriminate" bombing was aptly named: most of the bombs dropped on Nuremberg from 17,000 feet missed their target.

After much lobbying, led by Mike O'Loughlin, a colleague of Freeman Dyson, Bomber Command agreed to enlarge the hatch but the new design would not become standard until the very end of the war.

Moffat had one chance in seven of getting out of the plane alive.

The airmen who flew the Lancasters over Berlin accepted the air force propaganda that they could bail out alive. They also accepted the view that each raid on Berlin brought them one step closer to winning the most decisive battle of the war.

"What they were told was untrue," says Dyson. "By January, 1944, the battle was lost. I had seen the bomb patterns, which showed bombs scattered over an enormous area." German records support Dyson's contention that, far from being smart bombs, most were hit-and-miss. In one particular raid, bombers inadvertently hit 47 surrounding villages within a 30-mile radius of the intended target, Berlin.

"We merely showered incendiary bombs over the city," admits Dyson, "with a small fraction of high-explosive bombs to discourage firefighters. Important factories were protected by firefighting teams. Civilian housing and shops could be left to burn. Photographic reconnaissance a few weeks later showed factories producing as usual amid the rubble of burnt homes."

In February, 1944, Moffat's crew was sent to bomb Leipzig. The briefing for that mission forced him, for the first time, to confront the reality of what Bomber Command was doing.

"Normally they would say, you have a primary and a secondary target. Your primary target is the ball-bearing factory, or the submarine yards, or whatever. But this time, the primary target was the railway yards.

"The CO said, 'Okay, fellas, now you remember, the other night we bombed Berlin. Now all those people are on trains trying to get out of Berlin and they're going through the big railway centre.' That's when it hit me that we were actually choosing to bomb people instead of military targets.

"I thought, Oh my *God*! They're telling us to aim for these people as a primary target. I knew we had been killing people, accidentally, because there were bombs going off all over the place. There was no way we couldn't kill them. But that was the first time it drove home to me that it was Bomber Command's *aim* to kill people."

By spring, 1944, after five months of brutal raids, Bomber Command had failed to destroy the city of Berlin. Harris counted Hamburg and the Ruhr as successes, but "Victory Through Air Power" still eluded him. He had lost 953 bombers in 34 raids. And he knew that, after April 14, Bomber Command would be diverted to Operation Overload, the Allied code name for the invasion of Normandy.

On March 29, Moffat, Harvey and their squadrons were ordered on a final raid. The target was Nuremberg, one of Germany's oldest cities, the headquarters of the Nazi party and the hub of the world's toy industry.

"We came back from vacation," says Moffat, who had been on a week's furlough in Edinburgh with his navigator, Red Soeder, "and that night we were on ops. We looked at the target and, 'Oh my God!' Nuremberg — and in moonlight. Moonlight! We'd go to France and that's no problem; but to go into Germany in moonlight?"

Behind the scenes, one of Harris' advisors tried to talk him out of the mission, objecting that the clear, moonlit night would expose the bombers to terrible danger. A late weather report showed that the only cloud on the whole route hung over the target. Everyone expected the mission to be scrubbed.

It wasn't.

Nearly 6,000 airmen prepared for the attack.

It was Moffat's 10th mission, his skipper's 13th.

At approximately 10 p.m., March 30, 781 Lancaster bombers took off from the Yorkshire airfields in quick succession. The plan was for all the planes to bomb the target within a 20-minute period: a bombload dropped every one-and-a-half seconds.

The return flight to Nuremberg took eight hours. The crews could see the white vapour trails of the other aircraft in the stream.

"I was sitting at my tail gun and suddenly I saw the first Lancaster explode in a big, red, fiery ball," recalls Moffat. "It's the gunner's job to point out where aircraft go down. We started reporting the planes going down in flames, 'Aircraft going down in flames with no parachutes off the port.' This went on for 20 minutes. Twenty-one aircraft going down in 20 minutes. 'Aircraft going down in flames, no parachutes.' Finally the pilot said, 'That's enough, no more; don't give any more.'"

Through his cockpit windscreen, Harvey saw German fighters coming at him across the moonlit sky. Harvey was used to this: he had a gold watch, one of 12 awarded for dropping the most bombs on Berlin. But for the first time flying, he prayed.

He would have been even more terrified had he known that the Germans had two new secret weapons — a sophisticated tracking antenna that could guide a night-fighter, undetected, to the underbelly of a bomber. And an upward-firing gun called *Shrage Musik*. "A simple periscope gunsight was arranged so that the pilot could take careful aim as he flew quietly below the bomber's blind spot," says Dyson. "The main problem for the German fighter pilot was to avoid being hit by pieces of the exploding bomber."

Virtually the entire German night-fighter force — 200 planes — was deployed against the stream of approaching British and Canadian bombers. With the new German technology, 59 Lancs were shot down en route to Nuremberg. The crews never knew what hit them.

Miraculously, Moffat and his crew made it to the target. Most bombers, following the meteorological officer's windspeed miscalculations, flew off course and dropped their bombs northwest of Nuremberg, on the city of Schweinfurt. Moffat's plane dropped its bombs and headed home, but now their navigator was off course.

"So we turn 45 degrees to the port," says Moffat, "and the

pilot said, 'Okay, gunners, everyone keep your eyes open, we don't want to crash into anyone.' And every now and again, he reminds us, 'Okay gunners, you've got your eyes open, keep watch.' I couldn't see too well because I'm in the tail."

Suddenly, Moffat heard the pilot say, 'What the hell...' and then his head hit the turret so hard he was almost knocked out. He saw a plane drifting off to the rear, another Lancaster, one of their own, the only other aircraft in 40 miles. He called to the cockpit. No answer. He tried to open the doors to the main body of the plane, but they had crumpled shut. He signalled in Morse Code to the wireless operator. Silence. The plane seemed to be level. He had been in tough spots before; he decided to sit tight and wait it out.

"What I didn't know was that the plane was in a tail dive and I was on the inside of the spin so there was no centrifugal force.

"Then I noticed a tail fin missing and I realized what was happening."

Painfully, he uncurled his long legs and pushed open his turret. He was already wearing his parachute. He flipped on his back and rolled out. Still caught in the illusory weightlessness of the tailspin, he floated to earth in tandem with his plane. In a few moments, he'd be sucked into the plane's crash. The turret guns pointed at him. He had forgotten the safety catch, but he had no choice. He kicked against the guns to free himself from the deadly vacuum of the Lanc.

"It was just like God grabbed me and yanked me up real sudden. I heard the chute open. The idea had just gone through my head — I'm going to land in that clear field — when I hit the ground."

Moffat landed in Germany with nothing more serious than a nosebleed. For the next year and a half, he lived with the Resistance, the only man from the two crews to escape the collision alive. For him, the air war was over. He had flown ten missions as a gunner, and had never once fired his guns.

In one night, the raid on Nuremberg destroyed 108 planes. More airmen died — 545 — than in the entire Battle of Britain. In *Bomber Offensive*, the detailed wartime memoir of Air Vice Marshall Harris, which goes on at great length about Hamburg and Berlin, there is not a single mention of Nuremberg or the airmen who died.

INDISCRIMINATE BOMBING

To the very bitter end, Air Vice Marshall Harris believed his planes would cripple the German war machine, British casualties would be minimal and the German population would beg for surrender.

What really happened was this:

In May, 1942, Harris dispatched 1,000 planes to bomb Cologne; within two weeks, the city was back to normal.

In 1943, he ordered 207,600 tons of bombs dropped on Germany; that year, production of war weapons increased to 72,000. In 1944, bombing quadrupled to 915,000 tons; German war production that year increased to 105,258 weapons.

Not only was German morale undaunted but, according to Dyson, the destruction of their homeland at the end of the war gave the German people "the one thing that they lacked at the beginning, a clean cause to fight for." Goebbels couldn't have done a better job if he had created Bomber Command himself.

In the end, the real victims of the British air offensive were not only factories but families. German deaths from the air war are estimated at almost half a million (460,000), most of them women and children.

"When you saw those carpets of bombs, especially the incendiaries," says Moffat, "they looked like little diamond bracelets down there. I think the thing that saved most of us guys was that it was all so unreal."

At some point during their tour of duty, however, most airmen came to realize the awful intent of their missions. For Moffat, the realization had come at Leipzig. For Harvey, it was during the Battle of Berlin: "It was a very cold, clear night; snow on the ground. And it looked like a Christmas card scene down below. I hadn't seen that before. You could see the houses and the factories and the buildings. We dropped our bombs, and you could see the buildings going up, see the houses exploding, see the bombs going along the street, erupting and blackening the snow. Usually the target was obscured and you didn't get a good view of it. But to watch those houses going and to realize these were your bombs. It was very, very disturbing."

Once that realization dawned, a flyer had two choices — refuse to fly and bear the brand of Lack of Moral Fibre, or do as he was commanded. Air Vice Marshall Harris insisted he was just obeying orders:

The destruction seen from the air seemed unreal to the men in the planes.

"There is a widespread impression that I not only invented area bombing but also insisted on carrying it out in the face of the natural reluctance to kill women and children that was felt by everyone else. The facts are otherwise.

"Such decisions of policy are not made by Commanders-in-Chief in the field, but by Ministries, by the Chief of Staffs Committee and by the War Cabinet."

The British subscribed to the doctrine of "area" or "indiscriminate" bombing in which wars are won by delivering death and destruction from above. It was an appealing doctrine for two reasons: it avoided the bloody trenches of the First World War, and it offered the hope that war could be avoided by deterrence. If the enemy was frightened enough, went the theory, it would surrender, obviating hand-to-hand combat. Fifty years later, the doctrine persists in nuclear deterrents, "carpet" bombing and Star Wars defence.

"Bomber Command might have been invented by some mad sociologist as an example to exhibit as clearly as possible the evil aspects of science and technology," says Dyson. "The Lancaster, in itself a magnificent flying machine, was made into a death trap for the boys who flew it. A huge organization was dedicated to the purpose of burning cities and killing people. A bureaucratic accounting system failed utterly to distinguish between ends and means, measuring the success of squadrons by the number of sorties flown, no matter why, and by the tonnage of bombs dropped, no matter where."

Of the 125,000 air crew who served in Bomber Command, more than half — 73,741 — were wounded or killed. Fifty-five thousand died. One in every five was a Canadian. Relative to its population, Canada suffered the greatest loss of the Allied air forces: 9,919 pilots, navigators, flight engineers, bomb-aimers and gunners — the Brylcreem Boys, the Boys in Blue — most of them in their teens and early twenties.

One of those who died was Roger Fournier, the young French Canadian miner who signed up with Jim Moffat in Timmins, Ontario. Moffat and Fournier met up again, late in 1943, in Yorkshire, assigned to the same squadron.

"I was on duty that night," recalls Moffat.

"I said, 'Hi Roger, when did you get on the squadron?'

"He said, 'We arrived today.'

"So I said, 'I'll see you at four o'clock in the morning when you get back.'

"He never came back. They went across the coast, were shot down, and they were all killed. Their first trip.

"I wrote to his girlfriend. I didn't know what to say to the mother...

"See, they were the first French Canadian family that I was close with. The mother was jolly. And the grandfather played the fiddle and would do this tap-dance. We'd have a keg of beer and go on till midnight.

"When I got back, I went to see her. And she said, 'You came back, why couldn't Roger? Why did you survive and he died?' I agreed with her. I was no better, in fact I was a heck of a lot worse than some of the guys that didn't come back.

"She didn't necessarily hold it against me. But Roger was their only son. She just wanted me to explain it."

The Price of Victory: The Normandy Campaign

CHAPTER THREE

Major Phil Griffin crouched at the edge of a ripening wheat field in Normandy. Behind him waited over 300 men of The Black Watch — unshaven, exhausted, aching in boots that hadn't come off in weeks. They were among the thousands of Canadians who had landed in the June, 1944, Allied invasion of Normandy and who were now fighting their way across northern France, heading for the city of Falaise, and beyond that, Paris.

It was now the end of July and they were stalled at the foot of Verrières ridge. Their battalion commander was dead, killed by German machine-gun fire; their senior company commander, shot in the stomach.

Suddenly, 26-year-old Phil Griffin was in command.

He had joined The Black Watch elite of Montreal while studying postgraduate chemistry at McGill University. In his year's training in England, the college boy proved himself to his men — never asking a soldier to do anything he wouldn't do himself. Word of his competence spread through the Regiment. He was one of those officers the men would follow anywhere.

The soldiers of The Black Watch eyed Griffin anxiously, ready to advance. According to plan, the charge on Verrières ridge was to start at 5:30 a.m. But Griffin was waiting for tank support. According to plan, he was late. Through the hierarchy of the military, pressure built. Why wasn't he attacking?

Finally at 9:30 a.m., Griffin stood up in the waist-high wheat. He looked left, right, swung his arm in an arc and pointed forward. Behind him, the full battalion rose — two

Major Phil Griffin from Vancouver, British Columbia, at age 23. He joined The Black Watch Regiment in Montreal, while studying at McGill University.

The Black Watch Regiment of Montreal, 1944. Phil Griffin is in the front row, third from the right.

companies up, two companies back — and began its advance.

At first, there was silence except for the footfalls in the wheat. Amazed, the Germans watched the Canadians approach as if on parade. When The Black Watch was squarely in their gun sights, they opened fire — from the supposedly secure villages, with mortars; from machine guns, through sight-lines cut in the wheat; from the tanks atop the ridge.

One by one the Canadian soldiers fell, hardly firing a shot.

Griffin pressed on. Those few who could, followed. Only a runner turned back carrying the Major's message to the start-line: "Send no reinforcements."

In a last valiant push, Griffin ran up the slope to the crest of the hill.

THE BUILDUP IN BRITAIN

Bruce Ducat from Verdun, Quebec, in 1941.

On the pier at Greenock, Scotland's great North Atlantic port and wartime convoy base, a small crowd of Scots waved and cheered as Lance Corporal Bruce Ducat disembarked with several hundred other Canadians. Ducat, from Verdun, Quebec, had transferred to The Black Watch to get overseas fast so he wouldn't miss the action. Scotsmen ferried him and his Regiment ashore. Kilted pipers played them through the streets from the dock to the railway station. It was

September 3, 1940, and the soldiers of The Black Watch were on their way to war.

Ducat had joined a prestigious Regiment with a long military history. In Montreal, he had been piped into formation and lectured on the traditions of The Black Watch. On parade, he wore the Black Watch tam with its distinctive pompom of scarlet feathers — the symbolic "hackle," originally white, that the founding Black Watch had made red with the blood of their first kill, hundreds of years before. The Regiment had begun as a police force — a "watch" — of fierce lowland Scots, used by the British to control the Scottish Catholic tribes after the Battle of Culloden.

Now, the ranks of The Black Watch included the sons of Canadian Scots who lived in the moneyed core — the "Square Mile" — of downtown Montreal. And with Irish working-class boys like Ducat.

Jacques Dextraze, 21, from Montreal, Quebec, as an army cadet.

Jacques Dextraze signed up in 1940, in Montreal. He was 21, son of a French Canadian father and English Canadian mother. Concerned by Hitler's unchecked domination of Europe, he left his job at Dominion Rubber Company to join the infantry. Although many French Canadian nationalists wanted nothing to do with an "English war," Dextraze and thousands of young French Canadians joined up.

"My reasons were very simple," says Dextraze. "I'm listening to the radio and I'm hearing that this fellow Hitler is taking everything in Europe. He's imposing his law and his way of thinking on everybody. Then France fell. And I joined. I said, 'I've got to do my part. We've got to stop this guy.' I knew all kinds of things could happen to me — I had uncles who died in the '14-'18 war, three uncles on my mother's side killed. But I was ready to do it because there was a purpose, although it sounds kind of corny when you say that. Sure, I loved adventure, but I felt that there was a job to be done, and I felt that deeply."

Dextraze became a private in Les Fusiliers de Mont-Royal (FMR), the French-speaking equivalent to The Black Watch.

"We thought we were some kind of an elite. Really, we were no better than the Maisonneuves or any other French-speaking or English-speaking unit. But a lot of us thought we were better. Don't forget, when you're young, you like to think of yourself as the cat's meow.

"Then in 1942, Dieppe took place. FMR had a lot of casualties, so they sent me overseas. I was very happy. I phoned

Canadian Army recruits training in
England, 1941.

my wife who was on holidays — she was my fiancée then. We
met in Montreal, got married, stayed together ten days and
then I left for three years."

Dextraze arrived in the South Downs of England, a major in
command of a company of 130 infantrymen. In two years, he
had risen rapidly through the ranks, a skilled infantry
instructor, an officer with promise. He was only 23, but he
knew the military.

"A good soldier is a man who is physically fit; who knows
his weaponry — its characteristics and so on; knows how to
use ground; knows how to move; is disciplined and knows how
to obey. I trained my men to the ultimate, until I thought I had
done the very best I could."

The soldiers training in England marched all day with 80-
pound packs. At night, they used stunted spades to dig "slit"
trenches — six feet long, 30 inches wide and four feet deep —

Assault training at Aldershot, England, August, 1942.

to sleep in. Carrying packs, they practised using "flanking fire" to cover one another's advance.

Dextraze was turning civilians into soldiers. Canada had few men experienced in battle. In the English countryside, the young men learned what they could of war, adapting the special skills they brought from home. "We were good night-fighters," says Dextraze, "because in a country like Canada, young men from the city go to the country all the time or you come off a farm. We're used to darkness."

As a young boy, he had hunted with his father in the forests of Quebec, learning to use his senses to stalk game.

"Why are you afraid of darkness? It's because you can't see. You hear, but you can't interpret. It's all psychological. So put the guy in the night and get him to live with it, and find that it can be his ally."

Like its counterpart in chess, the infantry could move anywhere and take anything, Dextraze believed.

"It is not for nothing that the infantry is called the 'Queen of Battle.'"

Dextraze's father had been a strict disciplinarian and Dextraze dealt the same way with men only a few years younger.

"You've got no right to go out and amuse yourself," he drilled, "or piss around your time with the girls and the boys — taking a drink and so on. Use that time to prepare yourselves to do the job that we're going to have to do on the battlefield. Because one day, when the Big Book is opened, you're going to have to answer for this."

Deeply religious, Dextraze believed in what he was doing. "You've got to train yourself well. You've got to make necessary sacrifices so that you become professional at what you're doing. And then you've got to do it. And you've got to believe in God to help you to do the thing that you're supposed to do."

A soldier's soldier, Dextraze was always with his men.

"While you're under training, you eat the same food that they eat, you sleep under one blanket because they've only got one. They always remember this. When you go into action, they respect you. The soldier gives his life to a commander to do with what he wants. Can there be a greater gift than that? This is why a commander must always do all he can for his men. This is the only way that you can repay them for having made the ultimate sacrifice."

Thousands of Canadians were training at infantry bases in England and Scotland. Some had been there as long as five years, arriving in 1939 to fight with the British in France. In 1940, they were driven from the Continent when the Germans occupied France. Canadians remained in England as garrison troops. In 1941, when the United States entered the war, the Allies began to consider an invasion of Europe. In 1942, an initial attempt at Dieppe failed; of 5,000 Canadians who landed, 3,000 were killed, wounded or captured.

In 1943, the Allies prepared for a co-ordinated attack on occupied France. Training intensified for the Canadians in England. They scaled obstacles, cleared mine fields, embarked and disembarked, first from mock landing crafts built on parade grounds, then from real boats in Bracklesham Bay on England's south coast.

In the buildup during the winter of 1943-44, Viril "Bart" Bartlett, 21 years old from Truro, Nova Scotia, was shipped with his Regiment, The North Nova Scotia Highlanders, to the craggy north coast of Scotland. For three years he had been mostly at the huge infantry training camp at Aldershot. Now he trained, "crawling under wire, jumping in cold water, grabbing ropes, pulling yourself up rocks, waves crashing 75 to 100 feet below. It made us understand exactly what we would encounter. Prepared us for any eventuality."

At about the same time, Sydney Radley-Walters, 24, a farmboy

Viril "Bart" Bartlett, 21, from Truro, Nova Scotia, joined The North Nova Scotia Highlanders.

from the Gaspé, arrived in England. A varsity football player and university grad, he was second-in-command of a squadron of 19 tanks.

This war was the tank corps' debut: the Canadian Armoured Corps was only four years old. The five-man crews — driver, co-driver, gunner, operator and crew commander — were among 20,000 young men to graduate from the Canadian armour school between 1940 and 1945.

Radley-Walters began preparing his crews for combat. They engaged in mock battles — manoeuvring, taking aim, shooting blanks at each other across spare bits of British pasture, using training tanks because as late as January, 1944, only ten of the new Sherman tanks had arrived.

"And we couldn't drive tanks across a farmer's field because they needed the wheat," says Radley-Walters. "We had to stick to the roads. There was no live ammunition. We'd go to the ranges and do target practice, but it was unrealistic."

The tank crew trained almost daily with the infantry units they were to support.

Sydney Radley-Walters, 24, from the Gaspé, Quebec, en route to England.

"We lived and we ate and we drank with them," says Radley-Walters. "They were like brothers in arms. When you get close to people and you know them like that, well, when the time comes, you stick together. Nobody, but nobody, is gonna let the other guy down. That's the way we felt. Not only with the North Novas but also with the Hamilton Lights, the Stormont, Dundas and Glengarries. The longer you leave people together, the greater the reason for fighting."

By May, 1944, almost 3 million soldiers from the United States, England and Canada were drilling in the British countryside. Squadrons of planes buzzed overhead. Everyone, civilian and soldier alike, speculated about a joint British, United States and Canadian invasion of Europe. Where would we land? By air or by sea? What would we meet? An attack seemed imminent: but where? When?

On May 26, 1944, all military bases on the south coast of England were sealed. No one came or went without a special pass. Officers were briefed with bogus maps. "At long last," wrote one Regimental diarist, "this looks like the real thing."

Soon the theoretical "start lines" drawn on British soil would become villages and hilltops in France, defended by German troops. The Canadian soldiers were ready.

The North Novas landing craft en route to the Normandy beaches of France, June 6, 1944.

"We were keen as bloody mustard," says Dextraze. "We had trained so hard, the idea was to get on with it, you know. Gung ho and take it."

THE LANDING

From the deck of a Royal Canadian Navy ship in the English Channel, Radley-Walters watched the storm thrash the sea.

Soldiers eat K-rations during the day-long trip across the English Channel.

Around him, hundreds of ships tossed and pitched, through six-foot waves. After leaving Southampton, the officers had opened their sealed orders. The destination was Normandy, a stretch of sandy beaches on the northern coast of France. There would be five Allied landing points. The Canadian target was a five-mile beach code-named "Juno."

The storm was blowing itself out as Radley-Walters rocked in a landing craft eight miles out to sea. It was the morning of June 6, 1944. On the beach, the first wave of Canadians scrambled onto French soil. If they succeeded, another 14,000 would land before dark. On either side of them were the British, and farther west, the Americans — 130,000 Allied troops in all.

"In front, behind, on either side, the sea was completely covered with ships," says Radley-Walters. "We had a ringside seat on the run in — all of it going on in front. We went around in big circles, waiting our turn. That in itself was a bloody tricky naval manoeuvre, getting everybody in."

Unlike at Dieppe, the army now had full naval and air support, the first time all three arms of the Canadian military co-operated. Canadian mine sweepers helped clear the Channel of explosives. Bomber Command, including No. 6 Group, dropped more than 5,000 tons of bombs on the beach defences. British submarines flashed coloured lights to guide the boatloads of Canadian soldiers to their target.

"Practically everyone was sick," said Joseph LeBouthillier, a

Joseph LeBouthillier, 19, from Caraquet, New Brunswick.

Canadian soldiers land at Bernières-sur-Mer, Normandy, part of a five-mile beach code-named "Juno."

19-year-old Acadian fisherman from Caraquet, New Brunswick. "Three-quarters of the soldiers threw up. Me, I was used to the sea. Before I joined up, I fished for lobster and herring."

Poverty, not patriotism, had taken LeBouthillier and 40 of his buddies from New Brunswick's Lower Peninsula to this landing barge. The $25 a month the army offered was five times what he could earn at home, and he was fed and clothed, too. For one month in Canada, he had trained in Maritime wheat fields, without boots, wearing his Sunday sign-up clothes, barely understanding his English-speaking officers. Now, he was on one end of a gangplank leading to Normandy.

"I got the order from my officer to come last man off the boat. He says, 'Anyone refuse, you shoot.' But they all jumped off."

It was 8:05 a.m., the landing delayed by the storm. As LeBouthillier and the other Canadians waded through water up to their waists, artillery shells from the boats behind whizzed over their heads and exploded in the sand. Long-range shells from destroyers arced farther inland, destroying not only German defences but seaside cottages and village stores.

"When we finally got to the beach, everything was tremendous noise and smoke," recalls Radley-Walters. "As far as we were concerned, the infantry had already taken the beach. It was khaki with our dead."

Bodies from both sides were stacked like cordwood on the sand.

"And sitting down on their haunches were, oh, maybe three or four groups of German prisoners," says Radley-Walters. "The first Germans I had seen."

Outnumbered six to one, many Germans surrendered. A

The North Novas land on the beaches of Normandy with bicycles, June 6, 1944.

By the end of the first day, almost 20,000 Canadians had landed, taking the beach at a cost of almost 1,000 soldiers — dead, wounded or captured.

British sailor ferrying soldiers ashore watched Canadians march six of them behind a sand dune and, hoping to cadge a souvenir helmet, he followed. He found the Germans "all crumpled up. Every one of them had his throat cut. I turned away, sick to my stomach — I didn't get my tin hat."

Bulldozers rammed through sea walls that had been scaled with ladders and makeshift ramps by the first wave of infantry. Tanks fitted with rollers and chains flailed the fields, beating and exploding the surface mines to make way for the soldiers.

By the end of the morning, the Allies had landed.

Radley-Walters crawled over the debris — stones, bodies,

Bombs from planes and offshore
ships levelled seaside towns, but
further inland, French villagers
poured into the streets to greet
their Allied liberators.

tanks crippled by German guns. In the distance, he spotted the
landmark steeple of the Norman church dominating the
horizon — the designated assembly point for thousands of
Allied soldiers and their equipment. Radley-Walters rallied his
19 tanks and the "porpoise" that carried their ammunition.
The beach was a confusion of men and machines.

"We had to get inland fast and there was the world's biggest
traffic jam. Vehicles and tanks facing in all directions. Nothing
could move! What a mess! And in the middle of it all,
directing traffic, was Major General Rod Keller, commander of
the 3rd Canadian Infantry Division. I remember thinking,
maybe he should have been up front, getting us into Caen."

Newspaper reports of the invasion hailed it as an "easy and
unopposed landing." The Allies had "a toehold on the
Continent." The notorious "Atlantic Wall" had been
breached. Perhaps because casualties were only half as high as
predicted by the British War Office, it was hardly mentioned
that 9,000 men were killed, wounded or taken prisoner: 340
Canadian infantry killed, more than 500 wounded and 47
taken prisoner. LeBouthillier survived, but 125 men of his
North Shore Regiment were wounded or died. In St-Aubin-
sur-Mer, 90 percent of the buildings were rubble.

Infantrymen supported by tanks gradually moved south toward the French city of Caen.

By late afternoon, the traffic jam unsnarled and sunshine broke through the storm. Cheered by the soft light and the lack of resistance beyond the beaches, 1,000 infantry and 60 tanks — including Radley-Walters' squadron and Bartlett's North Nova Scotia Highlanders — pushed steadily south towards their first objective, the airport outside Caen. They kept to the road, a straight Roman causeway curiously sunken in the pastoral countryside, as if drawn by a giant finger at the beginning of time. On either side of the highway, steep banks edged fields that were sharply delineated by hedges of gnarled trees. *Bocage* was what the Normans called it — thick branches intertwined with generations of rocks. It slowed the Canadians down and dangerously obstructed American and British progress farther west.

"We would try to get some of the tanks and the infantry into the fields, but we'd run into the hedgerows," recalls Radley-Walters. "We could move in fairly good speed from one hedgerow to another, but then there was a barrier. And the hedgerows created positions for defence."

Outside Villons-les-Buissons, a village north of Caen, the *bocage* gave way to open fields and the Canadians camped for the night. Bartlett and his Regiment shovelled out slit-trench beds in an encircling fortress of tanks and sat down to their tins of rations. A few planes flew overhead. In the distance, men heard the occasional rumble of artillery. The night seemed calm enough.

Canadians examine a crippled
German tank for its weak points.

"I said to myself, ah, to hell," recalls Bartlett. "I went out in the open fields, pulled the wheat over me and went sound asleep. During the night, I was told later, they dropped parachute troops behind us. Either that or it was a lurking German behind. Anyway, this guy came across the field and jumped into my trench. Jimmy went out and captured him. Told me later the German had a knife in his mouth. Jimmy didn't even wake me up."

After years of training, the Canadians were seeing "action." Soldiers had drowned. Some were shot. A few had killed. But they had overcome the first line of German defence. Now they lay in their slit trenches, filled with exhilaration and dread.

"We knew the Germans were going to hit us soon," said Radley-Walters. "We could feel it."

COUNTERATTACK

From a corner turret of the medieval Abbey of Ardennes, nine miles from the beaches of Normandy, Kurt Meyer, commander of a regiment in the 12th SS Panzer *Hitlerjugend,* watched as the Canadians took to the road the next morning.

Meyer was 31. Around the neck of his camouflage uniform hung the honours he had won in battle — Iron Cross, First

Stuck in Hell's Corner, the Canadians, like this dispatch rider, spent much of their time dodging snipers.

Class, 1939; Knight's Cross, 1941; Oak leaves, 1943. At the Nuremberg Rally, he had been one of Hitler's personal bodyguards. He was in the front lines when Germany invaded Austria, Czechoslovakia, Poland and Holland. Like his fellow officers in the 20,000-man Panzer division, he was a hardened veteran of the ferocious Russian campaign.

At training camp, the Canadians had been warned about his regiment. "If you met a 12th *Hitlerjugend*," Ducat learned, "you were hitting real tough men who knew their job."

Under Meyer's command were teenagers, fresh from the fitness camps of the Hitler Youth, full of ideology and patriotism. Meyer was the patriarch they would follow and unquestioningly obey. One grenadier ran away to his family but was caught. Meyer boxed his ears, saying, "That's in place of your father."

On July 9, 1944, 33 days behind schedule, the Canadians finally crossed the river near Caen, rendered here in watercolour by Major W.A. Ogilvie.

Meyer watched as the Novies and the tanks pushed forward, extending the Allied line south toward Caen. He held his boys at bay until the Canadians were as isolated and exposed as a pointing finger.

After his three years of brutal fighting on the Eastern front, Meyer considered the Canadians *"kleine fische"* ... little fish.

At three o'clock on the afternoon of June 7th, the day after the Canadians landed, Meyer ordered a counterattack.

"By now we were getting a little tired," remembers Radley-Walters. "We got aboard on June 4th, were at sea all of June 5th, a lot of the guys seasick; June 6 we landed and we didn't have any sleep that night. We'd done our exercise in England and I think we were reasonably competent and confident that we could take them on and probably lick 'em. But we were all very tired."

Meyer's troops were fresh and eager, and they had superior weapons.

"The German machine guns fired close to 2,000 rounds a minute," Bartlett remembers. "Our Bren guns only fired 500. Theirs went 'Brrrrr...'; ours went 'put, put, put...'"

The German tanks — Panthers and Tigers — were huge, well-armoured, with powerful guns that could strike from a mile away. They could drive shells through the thin armour plating of the Canadian tanks at 4,200 feet per second, like a nail through an egg. The Allies' Sherman tanks were like Fords to the Germans' Mercedes. With an effective gun range of less than half a mile, most Shermans couldn't get close enough to the German tanks to shoot through their heavy front armour. Canadians had to aim for the thinner armour on the flank or the small space below the gun.

Travelling in the lee of a hedgerow, Radley-Walters saw 20 German tanks barrelling across the wheat field. They were the first he'd seen, and one was headed straight for him.

"He didn't know we were there, so we got the first shot away. On the second shot, we saw him start to burn. And, of course, everybody was tremendously elated until we saw a lot of ours start burning, too. And we realized that we were on the wrong side of the scale."

Radley-Walters saw the advancing German soldiers "firing like mad with their machine guns and rifles, the artillery from the enemy getting heavier and heavier. Our artillery, unfortunately, is not firing for the simple reason that we're out of range. We try to return the fire just as quickly as we can. And we're looking along hedgerows trying to pick out targets.

"Communications go out between the infantry and the tanks. We hear of a company of 100 men overrun in one place. We don't hear anything more from our reconnaissance troop; it gets wiped out."

Crouched in the fields, the Novies struggled to hold off the full force of Meyer's counterattack.

"Hundreds of them were coming at us through the wheat," recalls Bill Bailey, a 28-year-old Cape Breton miner who joined up with his brother, Don. "We just mowed them ones down, but the rest would step over 'em and keep on walking, like they were drugged. Of course, we were doing the same.

"Then this shell lands in the middle of us. It tore my pack right off. The guy on my left and the guy on my right both go down. I lean over the guy on my left, Fattenberg was his name, and he said, 'I'm dying, Bill.' I put my hand on him. I knew he was going, but I said, 'Hold on. I'll be back for you. But I gotta get the rest of the boys into town or we'll get cut to pieces out here.'

"We didn't have any shell fire to cover us so the Major orders us to pull back and take cover in an anti-tank ditch the

Germans had dug. As we're moving back, this captain comes along and tells us to stop and dig in. I say, 'I got orders to go back.' So he pulls a gun on me. I ignores him and motions for my men to dive for the ditch. Just then a German tank opens up and takes the captain's head clean off."

The tank battle was terrifying, even when the German volleys missed. "First one bounces maybe ten yards from you and this cloud of dust flies up," says Radley-Walters. "And right away, you think, the second one is going to get you. And of course, there's nowhere to hide. You're caught out in an open field."

After a three-hour battle — "one of our toughest, we were amateurs then," says Radley-Walters — the remnants of the Canadian advance troops fell back to the village of Les Buissons to hold their ground and assess their losses.

Of the Novies, 84 men died, including Bailey's brother, Don; 158 were wounded; 128 taken prisoner.

Of The Sherbrooke Fusiliers, Radley-Walters' Regiment, 26 were dead, 34 wounded.

The Canadians claimed they "killed" 12 of Meyer's tanks, but more than twice that many of their own were out of commission, 21 beyond repair.

"Everybody that could, snuck back; we tried to drain them for information," says Radley-Walters. "We knew very little then about who had survived. I don't think we went around wringing our hands or being terribly sad about all of this. We were just preparing to make sure that, by God, they weren't gonna push us any further back. Charlie Petch, who was commanding the North Novas, said, 'Okay, gang, we're gonna hold here.' And I think that sort of got us all together. And we said, 'By God, we are gonna hold. Nobody is gonna pass through here. By Gosh, we'd lost somebody in front, but nobody else is gonna come through us.' That inspired all of us. And it made us feel a little braver, too."

THE PUSH THROUGH HELL'S CORNER

Forced back from their objective, the Canadians entrenched at the village of Les Buissons. The Germans were at Buron, just a mile away. Here the two forces would stay, attacking and counterattacking, from early June, 1944, to early July, back and forth, for over a month.

They watched each other's every move, sniping and shelling

in a daily confusion of cat and mouse. Snipers aimed at each other across the road. To flush out the German snipers so they wouldn't "pick me off," one soldier put his helmet on his pack and showed it over the trench. "The helmet flew."

Bartlett remembers climbing a rooftop to spot a sniper.

"I stuck my head around the side of the chimney, looking. All of a sudden, splat. A sniper bullet hit just above my head. So I put my head around the other side, and I figured he might let one more, but not too many because he knows we'd be coming after him. So anyway, all of a sudden, this gun let go. Meech Mathenson was right below me. He says, 'Give me the co-ordinates on the map.' So I gave him the co-ordinates and he said, 'Stay there and let me know how close this comes.'

"So he gave the order and they fired the mortars. And my Lord, the mortars hit only about 50 feet from where the sniper gunfire was coming.

"So I stayed up. They blowed the next one — rained right down in there. I said, 'You're on target.' And then they just blasted the place with mortars."

Periodically, the daily sniping and shelling was interrupted by the co-ordinated infantry and tank assaults of half a dozen Canadian Regiments.

"We go first and the tanks come after. The infantry are always in front," says LeBouthillier. "There is nothing we can do when a man gets wounded. We have the order not to stop. The only thing we do is stick a rifle in the ground and put a helmet on top, so the tanks can see and not run over 'em. Then the stretcher-bearer comes."

The crux of the battleground was a crossroads marked on German military maps and under constant mortar and artillery fire. Around it, the trench warfare became tragically reminiscent of the battles on French soil a generation earlier. Casualties were so high that the Canadians nicknamed the area "Hell's Corner."

On July 9, 1944, 33 days behind schedule and after a month of bloody fighting, the Canadians reached Caen, the ancient city just beyond Hell's Corner. The liberation of Caen took two days and left 330 Canadians dead, 864 wounded — a heavier toll than D-Day.

In the two nights before liberation, almost 1,000 Allied bombers blasted Caen with 6,000 bombs in an effort to "clean out" Germans, almost all of whom had pulled out before the attack.

"When we got into the centre of Caen we couldn't move,"

The Canadians took Caen in two days of house-to-house fighting, which
left 330 Canadians dead and 864 wounded — a heavier toll than D-Day.

says Radley-Walters. "It was absolutely pounded to pieces. The rubble was 15 to 20 feet high. We took a couple of streets and bulldozed them completely so that vehicles could get through."

A month later, Donald Pearce, an infantry platoon commander with the North Novas, would write, "It is as though the place had been lifted bodily a mile high in the air, turned over at this point, and allowed to drop straight down to earth again. We passed other shelled towns and villages, all without signs of life, and wondered ironically if this is what they meant by liberating a town; they must mean liquidating."

The centre of the 1,000-year-old city was destroyed in 40 minutes. No German bodies were found. Over 300 citizens of Caen died. The only part of the city spared was an "island of refuge" around the Abbaye-aux-Hommes, where the French Resistance had warned the British there would be thousands of civilians gathered.

What was left of the population of Caen poured into the streets to greet their liberators.

"These are Canadians, of all the Allies the closest to us; many of them speak French," wrote a local historian. "The joy is great and yet restrained. People — the sort of people who considered the Battle of Normandy nothing but a military promenade — have reproached us for not having fallen on the necks of our liberators. Those people forget the Calvary that we had been undergoing since the 6th of June."

The Canadians, too, had been undergoing their own Calvary. Between landing in Normandy on June 6 and the operations of late July and August that cleared the way to Paris, the Canadians fought a desperate series of battles north and south of Caen, all 18 Canadian infantry battalions suffering heavy losses. For the first few weeks, reinforcement troops were well trained, but as the battle wore on, the replacements were less and less prepared.

"Most of the men we're getting are soft," said Harry Foster, commander of the 7th Infantry Brigade. "They have been trained to cook, bake, drive, type and shuffle papers. Everything but kill Germans. The problem is with the bloody politicians in Ottawa who don't realize that in war men are wounded and die and have to be replaced."

Canadian Prime Minister Mackenzie King had won a referendum endorsing conscription in 1942, but he would not invoke mandatory enlistment until November, 1944. In the meantime, Canadian ranks rapidly thinned: for every two men killed or wounded, there was only one trained soldier to take their place.

Donald Pearce, an infantry platoon commander with the North Novas, flaunted army regulations and kept a journal of his war experiences.

A Canadian soldier priming hand grenades before an attack. A constant reserve of men available to replace those killed in battle, proved to be one of the Allies' primary military advantages.

Nevertheless, the slow stream of raw recruits would eventually tip the balance in the Battle of Normandy. The Allies outclassed the Germans in artillery, air power and munitions, and they had an open route to supplies stockpiled in England. The Germans had superior tanks and guns but their supply line for food, ammunition and reinforcements was 400 miles long and constantly under attack by Allied bombers and Resistance saboteurs. After five years of fighting, the German soldiers were experienced, but the Fatherland was hard pressed to replace them when they died. Having a large cache of men to take the place of those killed on the front lines was the Allies' primary military "advantage."

"The disadvantage is that you're brought back to strength with men who've never fought before," says Radley-Walters. "You're getting a lot of greenhorns and amateurs."

After one battle, Radley-Walters was sent nine new lieutenants to replace men he had lost. In the dark behind the front lines, he tried to condense two years of training into minutes.

"So we sat under a tree with a little flashlight and I took some rocks out of my pocket and said, 'I've been here for a month or so. Here's how I operate. I put four tanks there, and four tanks there. Of those four, I put two up like this, and I move the one in the centre and when I get up to here, I bring the back ends up here. And this is how we do it on withdrawal. Now you understand that? What I'm going to do is put you over here with these four little rocks. And you're going to be this one and you're going to be that one and so on.'

"That's the time I had. And two of those men were killed the next day. I know their names now when I look at our honour roll. But I certainly didn't know them then.

"How the hell do you get to know your people when you get a hundred tonight and you're committed the next day to a very violent battle? How can you put them into action at four o'clock the next morning and pretend that there is any semblance of order or control? We were just told to keep on going and keep on going."

Experienced soldiers were valuable. When wounded, they were returned to the battlefield as soon as possible. LeBouthillier, hit in the back with shrapnel, was sent to a hospital in England. After two weeks, when his wounds were still too raw to support a pack, an officer told him that he was going to France for two months of convalescence. "He said I'd be better off because it was French there. I believe him. I go off

Few dying soldiers had the benefit of last rites. Some men that died forward of the front lines were not buried for a month, and some not at all.

During a lull in the battle, these men rest while holding a bridge at Benouville.

The trench warfare around Caen
became tragically reminiscent of
the First World War.

to France and that very evening I'm back with my company on
the firing line."

On the battlefield, the tank crews suffered their own particular
hell.

"If a tank gets hit you jump out if you're alive and can still
move," says Radley-Walters. "We figured, from experience,
that if you're in a diesel, you had about 14 seconds, for the
driver, co-driver, gunner, operator and you. With a gas engine,
8 to 9 seconds. And in some cases you're blown right out of the

bloody tank. The greatest fear we all had was fire. We weren't worried as much whether we were gonna lose arms or get killed. We worried about getting burnt. And that's what happens in a tank. It burns, for a long time. All day."

The Germans called the Sherman tanks "Ronsons" because they burned so well.

It didn't take the tank crews long to realize they would have to beef up their Shermans if they wanted to survive. Just as they had fiddled with their pickups to give them more zip on Canada's back country roads, so they jerry-built their tanks. Crews scrounged track from disabled Panthers and Tigers and spot-welded the metal over the hull of their Shermans. The homemade chain mail protected Radley-Walters' tank for nine hits. When word spread of the strange gear, military experts arrived for inspection. They looked at the customized tanks and asked Radley-Walters if he knew what he was doing.

"And I said, 'Sure I know what I'm doing.'

"They said, 'Well, you've added about four tons on the vehicle.'

"And I said, 'What does that matter?'

"And they said, 'Well, those tracks that you've got on there will probably only go about another 500 miles. And those engines, they'll only turn over for about another 500 hours.'

"And I turned and I pointed to a ridge we'd been walking back off a few times and I said, 'Look, if this thing will go from here to the top of that bloody ridge she's paid for herself.'"

As the summer heated up, Canadian soldiers stripped off their heavy wool uniforms and did battle without the encumbrance of inappropriate clothing. Unorthodox, resourceful, they did what they had to, adapting as they went.

As supplies dwindled, every tank, however badly damaged, was salvaged from the battlefield and brought back behind the front lines for repair. One night, after hearing a motor running all day, Radley-Walters snuck out to get a tank.

"I found the crew commander dead in the bottom of the thing. A round had come through and struck him in the head and killed him instantly. I thought it was just going to be a simple job of putting a rope around him and pulling him up through the turret. But rigor mortis had set in. He was like a doughnut. There was no way to get him out but to take a machete and cut him in half. We had to take him out in two pieces and we buried him. But when we got the tank back, because of the blood and muck and so on in the bottom of it,

Casualties were heavy on both sides.

the men didn't want to crew it again. They'd crew anything else, but they didn't want to crew one where a man had been killed.

"They called it a 'Jonah.' There was the scent of death in it."

Death permeated the battleground. The fields were littered with bodies — carcasses of horses used to pull the German artillery, bloated bodies of dairy cattle abandoned by fleeing farmers, the rotting corpses of British, Canadian and German soldiers.

Jacques Dextraze arrived at the front lines in mid-July. And the sight of one dead soldier imprinted itself indelibly on his mind.

"I can see it today, a German at the corner of a crossroad, flat just like a sheet of paper. And tanks and trucks and so on were passing over it. And the dust, you know. And I can still see the corner and see this human body there."

"Nobody was burying their dead forward of the front lines," says Radley-Walters. "There were a lot of North Novas dead, a lot of engineers, a lot of Canadians and Germans, too. Some troops weren't buried for a month. It was extremely hot. And the smell was, it was horrible, really. The absolute stink as you went by was overpowering.

"The smell of death is very peculiar — very, very sweet. It affects you. One night when we had a little bit of time and the padres couldn't get out, I started burying the infantry dead, digging a shallow grave and putting them in and marking them. The smell of death got on my clothes and sort of stayed. I went down to a brook and I washed my hands over and over again. I put water on my battle dress, but I still stunk.

"And I decided on my own that none of the crews or myself should get involved in that again. I said, 'That's it, we'll stand

Captured German soldiers. The minute an enemy surrendered, a soldier was enjoined to respect and protect the man he had just tried to kill. Not surprisingly, both Canadian and German POWs died at the hands of their captors.

the horror outside. Let somebody else do it.' Because if you got to pick up your buddy and dig a hole and bury him, I think it turns you against the type of things that, as a soldier ... I just don't think you ever get used to it."

Few soldiers could handle the horror indefinitely. So many were dead — friends, buddies they had trained and joked with for years. Like brothers. Family. Like themselves. The young cooks, drivers and clerks shoved into the line didn't know anyone and no one knew them. The comradeship built in training was seeping out with the blood of those killed.

Rum was sometimes issued during foul weather or before battle, and many men augmented the army ration with Calvados, the fiery apple brandy of Normandy.

A few men drank themselves blind. Some urinated and defecated in their pants when the battle started.

Men on both sides lost their humanity.

"Around the 7th or 8th of June some 12th SS infiltrated the forward positions of the Regiment de la Chaudière — who were pretty tough boys," recalls Leo Gariepy, a Canadian officer. "The Chauds went mad in the night battle. They slit the throats of most Germans they found, wounded as well as dead. I saw the carnage from my tank. Officers had to draw their pistols against their own men to make them stop."

Immediately after landing on D-Day, 18 Canadian soldiers had been taken to the courtyard of Meyer's headquarters at the

Abbey of Ardennes. One by one, they were shot in the head.

These massacres were not isolated incidents. The Canadian army estimates that 134 Canadian POWs were murdered by the 12th SS during the Battle of Normandy. In one case, German trucks drove through columns of prisoners. An eyewitness reported a truck running over POWs, crushing legs and breaking backs.

Each act of savagery fed the next. A German division doctor found ten *Hitlerjugend* dead in a semicircle, a medic still holding a dressing to his wounded comrade. They had been shot by Canadians or British. German soldiers took revenge by shooting Canadian prisoners.

The morality of war was confusing. Dextraze told his men, "Your job is to kill the enemy. That's your principal job. But the minute an enemy comes out with his hands up in the air, you must respect him and you must protect him."

Dextraze felt responsible for the prisoners he took, but he couldn't always protect them. Once, after taking a small village by surprise, he rounded up 85 German soldiers.

"I select an officer to take them back to the POW cage. He goes back, making them run to the bridge that we had come over. These prisoners had already been running for a couple of miles when they came to the bridge. 'No, no, you don't take the bridge, you swim.' Now these guys fell into that water and most of them drowned. I felt very bad when I saw them all piled up beside the bridge."

Later, when he found he had to withdraw, Dextraze simply left 30 other prisoners behind.

"I didn't talk to them. I didn't look at them or anything. I left them in the hole that they were in and I withdrew. What happened to them I don't know. But this was a hell of a lot easier for me, as a man, with my conscience, to let these guys, you know, fare for themselves. I couldn't shoot them. I couldn't find the guts to shoot them."

After the war, in Canada's first war crimes trial, Kurt Meyer was convicted and sentenced to death for the murder of the Canadian POWs at the Abbey, a penalty later commuted to life imprisonment. No Canadian soldier in Normandy was ever investigated for killing German prisoners, although the horrifying truth is that there was murder on both sides.

As Jacques Dextraze says, "This happens in war."

VERRIÈRES RIDGE

In the two weeks following the liberation of Caen, the Allies pushed the Germans three miles south of the city to a horseshoe of high ground known as Verrières ridge. Bounded by the Orne River on the west, the gentle slope cradled the villages of St. Martin, Verrières and Tilly-la-Campagne. More important, it straddled the intended Anglo-Canadian route south to Falaise and eastward to Paris.

The Germans assumed this route would carry the main thrust of the Allied attack. On a critical sweep of high ground, seven full German divisions dug in.

"As we moved out from Caen, we were being constantly shelled and mortared," says Radley-Walters. "The German observation points were absolutely excellent. They could dominate the ground over which we were going to come. We knew it was going to be held fairly heavily."

On the morning of July 20, after a downpour, 24-year-old Jacques Dextraze led his company of 120 Fusiliers in an initial push toward Verrières ridge. Dextraze's immediate objective: a farm called Beauvoir nestled at the base of the slope. It was his first major battle.

"Inside, your heart is ... cataboom ... cataboom ... but you can't show that you're scared. So I lit my pipe and marched. The next thing I know I'm smoking a cigarette. Now I've got a pipe and a cigarette going.

"Then I hear this buzzing around my legs. I look down through the waist-high wheat and think, 'Wasps.'

"They weren't wasps. They were German bullets. Just before the farm, artillery and mortar shells started falling on top of us.

"In a few seconds, I lost most of my company. They never had a chance to fire a shot."

Dextraze and a few other survivors crept back to the Fusiliers' line.

"But the guys there were so nervous they started shooting at us, thinking it was the enemy, and I said, 'Hey, *qu'est-ce que tu fais là?*' And then they knew we weren't Germans, and we were let in."

After two major attacks and four days of fighting, the ridge remained in German hands. Gradually, the Canadians — among them The Black Watch, the Novies and the Fusiliers — gained the ground and villages leading up to it. "You'd be in one house and clear the Germans out and you'd move into the next house and they'd go back into that first house that you

In the assault on Verrières ridge, July 25, 1944, only one in seven objectives was taken. Almost 1,200 Canadians were killed or wounded, including virtually all of The Black Watch under Phil Griffin's command.

just cleared," says Radley-Walters. "I don't think they were ever completely cleared out of those little villages."

The narrow swath of farmland and towns would cost the Canadians 1,524 wounded, 441 dead. Still, Dextraze felt they were winning the war. "What the hell do you think. We were young bloody punks ready to believe any damned thing. We didn't get killed — so we won!"

In the last week of July, General Guy Simonds ordered a third attack on Verrières ridge. Fresh from command in the successful invasion of Italy, Simonds was the new General Officer Commanding of the 2nd Canadian Corps — two infantry divisions, 14 artillery Regiments and an armoured brigade.

"We are ordered to be on notice to move," wrote the North Novies' Regimental diarist. "This is indeed a mental blow and is felt by all ranks. We need a rest and refit, having been in the line since D-Day. The men and officers are looking worn out."

Many were stretched to their limits.

"A shell bounced off our trench," says Ducat, "and within minutes we had three guys go wacky. One an officer, one a corporal and one a private. The officer — God, he was a big man — just broke down and cried. Had to get him out quick. The private jumped out of the trench and started running circles in a pasture until one of the guys tackled him, then got him back to the aid post."

The night before they were to attack Verrières ridge, Ducat was sent out on patrol with six new replacements from England.

"Three o'clock in the morning and we get close enough to some Germans to hear them whispering. Two of the kids with me just go to pieces, they're so scared. I got them back to the Regimental Aid Post where there was a doctor."

Ducat returned to the trenches at 3 a.m. "I was tired, I was fed up, and I was bloody mad. Going out with six new men on a standing patrol. They should be able to hack that, just going out on standing patrol."

Many couldn't. By the end of the Normandy campaign, "psychiatric collapse" would account for almost one in every three casualties.

At 3:30 a.m. on July 25, 1944, Simonds' closely timed attack on Verrières ridge began. It was code-named "Spring," the last, but not the least costly, operation of the long "holding attack" in which Canadians and British occupied the Germans while the Americans pushed through western Normandy into Brittany.

In all, 32,000 Canadians in more than 30 Regiments were massed for "Spring," each Regiment with its own target on the ridge. The ridge itself was about three miles long, half a mile wide and about 230 feet high — a short, sharp climb of 30 feet and a 300-foot open rise to a wooded crest at the top. At the base, it fanned out into wheat fields spotted with

A Canadian soldier guards a German prisoner at Caen railway station. By the end of the Normandy campaign, 200,000 Germans were taken prisoner.

mining and farming villages.

The 3rd Canadian Infantry Division — including Bartlett and The North Nova Scotia Highlanders — would attack the ridge east of the road.

The 2nd Canadian Infantry Division — including Ducat and The Black Watch — would attack Verrières ridge west of the Falaise road.

By dawn, having "cleared" St. Martin and St. André, The Black Watch crouched in the wheat fields, ready to begin the push up the slope.

Their battalion commander had been killed in St. Martin. Their senior company commander was fatally wounded. Command of The Black Watch now fell to 20-year-old Major Phil Griffin.

A good officer, Griffin had his battle procedure down pat. Secure your flank: the village streets and rooftops were reported clear; to double-check, he sent out his own patrols. Attack with artillery: shelling had pounded the ridge long ago; if he didn't move out soon, he would have to reset the artillery barrage. Wait for tank support: well, he was waiting.

But the day was brightening. The tanks had not come. The attack was four hours behind schedule and the pressure was mounting, bearing down on Griffin with the full force of the Allied chain of command.

"Terrible pressure on him," says Radley-Walters, "the pressure on him when his commanders got killed and everybody's yelling, 'Move on! Push on! What's holding you up? What's wrong with you? Get going!' And orders coming from fairly senior, like brigade headquarters, saying, 'Get going! Get going!' And you're a major and you're in action for the first time and you're believing, 'Jesus, I better get going. Brigadier's after me. Everybody's after me.'"

Griffin decided not to wait any longer. He gave the signal and more than 300 men, including Ducat, followed him through the open wheat fields toward the ridge.

"Lord loving God, there's something wrong," Ducat noticed immediately. "There's no covering artillery fire. Never in all our rehearsals in England did we attack like this. We lined up and followed like sheep."

Exhausted from a night of skirmishes, carrying packs heavy with ammunition, they plowed through the waist-high wheat.

Suddenly, all hell broke loose.

"Tex Richard, an American buddy in the Watch, was right beside me when a shell blows him up," recalls Ducat. "He says, 'Duckie, come help me!' I says, 'I can't, but I'll be back, Tex, sure as hell.' But we weren't allowed to stop. And the stretcher-bearers never got to him. He just bled to death.

"We were like one big family, the unit. A lot of us had been together for four years, real friends, real buddies. And then you see them go ... and there's not a bloody thing you can do."

On the wheat field, The Black Watch fell by the score, mowed down by machine guns, blown up by artillery and mortar shells. The noise was deafening. The smell of cordite from the bombs was like a deadly perfume.

"Good God, this is it," thought Ducat. "If we make it out of here we're going to be bloody lucky today. This is going to be a rough one."

The Germans were more in control of the area around the ridge than the Canadians realized. The villages seemed "clear" because the Germans had held their fire when Griffin's patrols

Fresh from commanding the successful invasion of Italy, General Guy Simonds arrived in Normandy to take command of the 2nd Canadian Corps, orchestrating their push towards Paris.

checked the streets. They had hidden replacements in the mining tunnels and air shafts flanking the Black Watch positions, camouflaged tanks under haystacks, set up machine guns at the end of sight-lines mown through the grain.

They watched the Canadians advance and could not believe what was coming toward them.

"The soldiers were marching upright, holding rifles across their breasts in readiness, as if on a drill square," recalls a Panzer officer who witnessed the battle. "Waves of men rolling steadily forward, no sign of panic despite their visible losses. This was most impressive and perplexing."

When the Canadians were within killing range, the Germans opened fire. Hardly a bullet missed. "They did not go for cover but kept on marching upright. To us, soldiers with four or five years of experience in Russia, this was an almost unreal sight. After the first rounds from our tank cannon, we actually got scruples about firing on these Canadians lacking cover or defence weapons. But we continued to give flanking fire from the machine guns on three tanks."

Griffin pressed on to the crest of the ridge. Hundreds of bodies littered the wheat field. Only 60 men still followed.

"When we got up there, we weren't walking anymore," says Ducat. "We were running, charging, wanting to get out of this murderous fire coming down on us."

Someone yelled at Griffin, "We can't go on. It's murder to go on."

There was no thought of turning back.

"We were Black Watch," says Ducat. "We never learned the word 'retreat.' And I didn't want to be branded a coward. I didn't want to bring disgrace on my family, on my Regiment."

Behind him, in the distance, Ducat heard the rumble of Canadian tanks, out of communication with the battalion, the wireless set knocked out at the beginning of the charge.

Griffin dispatched a runner. "Tell them to send no reinforcements."

Moments later, Phil Griffin, "a good and honest soldier," was blown up.

"The last picture I remember is a few Canadian soldiers, mostly wounded, trying to get north," recalls the eyewitness. "No fire was directed to these retreating soldiers. We had been too deeply impressed, and embarrassed, by this sacrifice and gallantry of a battalion which had no chance against our position, no close air support and meagre artillery. It had been, well, sheer butchery. I think the dominating feeling was, 'Let

these poor blokes get home safely.'"

It was a brief, violent battle — over in less than an hour. Except at Dieppe, no other Canadian battalion in the Second World War suffered such casualties. The prestige of The Black Watch prompted an investigation by the Canadian Minister of Defence, but the Black Watch carnage was not unique. Except for Dieppe, more Canadians died on July 25 than on any other day in the Second World War.

Ducat was "blown up in the air, come down on my face, blood spurting out my arm." Captured and sent to POW camp at Reims, he was later liberated by the United States Army. Of the over 300 Black Watch soldiers sent to take Verrières ridge, fewer than two dozen made it back to the Canadian lines alive.

On the other side of the road to Falaise, The North Nova Scotia Highlanders were ordered to take Tilly-la-Campagne and the high ground beyond.

To make it possible to fight 24 hours a day, Simonds used "artificial moonlight" — huge searchlight beams bounced off clouds to light the soldiers' way. On the night of the attack on

At Tilly-la-Campagne, casualties were so high and the surviving soldiers so exhausted, that the brigade commander refused to order them into battle. He was subsequently relieved of his command.

Tilly, the sky was clear.

"When we started off," says Bartlett, "these damned lights went on behind us. They more or less silhouetted everybody. We walked through our own shadows. It was eerie. Any smart German officer, all he had to do was line up his artillery and fire. My God Almighty, it was all hell, to tell the truth."

Once again, the Germans had slashed the field with machine-gun trenches. Once again, haystacks turned into tanks.

"The Germans were shouting, 'Come and get it, Canada. Surrender, Canada.' Oh, I'll never forget Tilly, the moaning and the dead all around."

By dawn, Bartlett had lost half his Novies. Those left were pinned down, contact with battalion command severed. They dug in, fired their remaining ammunition and when darkness finally fell, they retreated.

The Division Commander, Major General Rod Keller, ordered Brigadier Dan Cunningham, commander of the 9th Brigade, to go back and attack Tilly again. Cunningham passed the order on to the North Novas, the Stormont, Dundas and Glengarries.

Commanding officers, Petch of the Novas and Christiansen of the Highlanders, told him their battalions weren't up to it. "Casualties," explains Cunningham. "They'd been fighting since the 6th of June. The battalions were weak." Out of loyalty to his battalion commanders, Cunningham listened to what they had to say, and then went to assess the situation. The North Novas had 61 killed, 46 wounded, 32 taken prisoner. He saw "companies down to 10 or 12 men, a lot of wounded. They just were tired out. They needed to go out and rest, not to fight." Cunningham heard and saw enough to convince him that "the brigade wasn't fit to go into action." It was a difficult decision but he returned to Keller's headquarters to tell him the attack was off.

Less than a month before, Keller had been judged by a British superior as "not fit tempermentally and perhaps physically" to command a division. Admitting fatigue, he asked that he be relieved of command on medical grounds. Simonds refused, citing the negative effect that a change of command would have on troop morale. Keller stayed. Now he was faced with troops that wouldn't fight and an ex-student refusing to obey orders. Keller and Cunningham exchanged harsh words.

"He thought they could do it and I thought they couldn't,"

says Cunningham.

"He said, 'You know if we don't go I'll lose my job and so will you.'

"And I said, 'I don't give a ... I'll go back to practice law.'"

The Novies and the Highlanders stayed put. Simonds called off the attack on the ridge.

Within days, Cunningham was relieved of his command. So were Christiansen and Petch.

"There is courage in taking your sword out," says Dextraze, "going over the parapet and bashing right and left and firing your gun and so on. But there is also the moral courage of standing on your two feet, assessing a situation and saying, 'No, this can't go on; this can't go on!'"

In the assault on Verrières ridge on July 25, 840 Canadians were wounded; 362 killed. Of the seven "objectives" on Verrières ridge, only one was taken.

This was war.

And it *was* going on. And on.

THE ROAD TO FALAISE

Midnight, August 8. A gigantic cloud of dust swirled up from behind the Allied lines. Fifty thousand men — Canadian, British, Polish — thousands of vehicles, hundreds of tanks, were on the move.

The ridge had thwarted the first attacks, but Simonds had devised an intricate "set piece" that would co-ordinate the assault potential of infantry, armour, artillery and air forces.

In the first phase, over 1,000 RAF heavy bombers would bombard the Germans in their fortified villages, followed by a barrage from 400 guns. Under artificial moonlight, the corps would burst out with the tanks and infantry. The infantry would be ferried through the deadly German defensive fire by a new Simonds invention, "kangaroos" — jerry-built carriers, forerunners of the armoured personnel carriers that would become a battlefield staple in the 1960s.

In the second phase, just as the Germans prepared to counterattack, Simonds would stop the push and bomb them again: 700 planes from the U.S. 8th Air Force.

In the third phase, tanks would seize the high ground overlooking Falaise, the ancient home of William the Conqueror.

The operation was code-named "Totalize." Strategically, it

For both Canadians and Germans, this was a war of teenagers. Most soldiers were under the age of 25.

was designed to take this key German defence, open the way to Falaise, and if possible, link the Canadians with the Americans.

The Canadians, British and Poles massed in tight columns of vehicles on either side of the Falaise road, the "kangaroos" sandwiched between the tanks. Radley-Walters walked from the front to the back of the line without once setting foot on the ground — half a mile of armoured vehicles were ready to go.

The signal was given. The tanks rolled out. Searchlights bounced off the clouds to light the way to the ridge, their beams diffused in a haze of mist and dust.

The Germans opened fire.

"They had smokeless ammunition," says Radley-Walters, "but when they fired their weapons, there was a spark that came off the muzzle of the gun. If you were smart enough and looking in that particular area, fine, you locate their equipment. Move towards that spark. All I can remember seeing is sparks and the fall of the shot in front of us. Move towards the spark, keep moving."

By morning, the Canadians had barrelled through the German defence line. German infantry were surrendering by the dozens.

"The Brits were coming up on our right. In front of us was beautiful, open, rolling country," remembers Radley-Walters.

Phase One had worked. The Canadians pushed forward, without much resistance, towards Falaise. At noon, halfway to the city, the tanks ground to a stop. That was the plan: at 12:30, the road would be bombed.

Only Kurt Meyer and the remnants of the 12th SS stood between the Allies and Falaise.

"My knees were trembling. The sweat was pouring down my face," said Meyer. "I realized that if I failed now and if I did not deploy my division correctly the Allies would be through to Falaise and the German armies in the West completely trapped. I knew how weak my division was, and the double task which confronted me at that time gave me some of the worst moments I ever had in my life."

Shortly after noon, the United States Air Force bombed the field on either side of the Falaise road in front of the Canadian line. One lead bomb-aimer, badly wounded, dropped his bombs too soon, hitting Allied troops. Eleven planes followed suit. Another bomber group mistook the target: 65 Polish soldiers were killed; 250 wounded. The hardest hit Canadian unit was The North Shore Regiment: 100 dead.

"To be bombed by the enemy is bad," wrote the Regimental Chaplain. "To be hit by your own bombers is worse."

"We took hours to untangle the mess in our lines from the bombing," says Radley-Walters. "Soon as we're ready to move, I see coming about 20 tanks, Panthers and Tigers. They're counterattacking two Canadian armoured divisions. Well, we kill about a dozen of them and the rest fall back. But it works. They give us a bloody nose, the big attack is delayed again, and it's getting dark."

To make up for lost time, Simonds ordered the tanks to press on through the night.

The British Columbia Regiment, the BCR, newly arrived at the front and eager for their first battle, was to have its tanks in position by dawn at Point 195, a knoll west of the road, just outside Falaise.

At 3 a.m., the crews pulled out through the mist into a landscape virtually devoid of landmarks. Fifty tanks carrying 200 infantry skirmished sporadically, eventually passing a village that seemed quite like the one on their map. "High ground sighted," recorded the Regimental war diarist enthusiastically, "and we headed for it."

Shortly before 7 a.m., almost on schedule, the tanks reported back to headquarters: objective less than a mile away; awaiting reinforcements.

At about the same time at Meyer's headquarters, German reconnaissance reported a small Canadian tank force on the high ground just outside Falaise.

By 8:30 a.m., five German Tigers from the west and ten Panthers from the east flanked the BCRs and destroyed ten of the Canadian tanks.

The Canadian tank colonel radioed for artillery fire and asked again for reinforcements — German tanks 650 yards to the southeast.

Headquarters ordered artillery fire and radioed back to the tanks — did they hit the target?

No response. Wireless dead.

By 9:30 a.m., 22 Canadian tanks were destroyed, many men shot and burned — German infantry and tanks attacking in force, very urgent medical needs.

No communication. A reconnaissance plane flew over Point 195. The crew saw nothing. Tank reinforcements left from headquarters, but they were ambushed on the way.

The BCRs loaded their wounded into infantry half-tracks and made it past the German tanks back to the Canadian line. More tanks were sent to Point 195.

At 2 p.m., soldiers in the BCRs cheered Polish tanks they saw in the distance. The tanks fired on them, thinking they were Germans. The BCRs sent up recognition smoke. The tanks stopped but they couldn't reach the soldiers. British planes flew over and fired on the Germans. God, how the men cheered.

Neither the tanks nor the planes reported the position of the BCRs.

4:30 p.m. Tanks are burning furiously, many with dead crews in them. Men are cracking; running out of morphine and bandages.

"I saw one soldier, shot through the thigh and with a broken leg, still throwing grenades," reported an officer. "Every man who was still conscious was firing some sort of weapon. Lieutenant Colonel Worthington was killed by an exploding German mortar bomb."

Cut off and alone.

By the time the Canadians reached Falaise, the 20,000-man 12th SS was reduced to less than 500 soldiers scattered throughout the city's ruins. The Germans had to be ferreted out in savage house-to-house fighting.

The British Columbia Regiment had taken a wrong turn in the dark.

They were on the other side of the road, miles away from Point 195. Utterly, hopelessly lost.

By mid-afternoon, 47 of the 50 tanks were destroyed. Forty men were dead, 38 wounded and 34 would soon be taken prisoner. At dusk, as the final German attack began, some surviving BCRs made for the Allied lines. The rest simply surrendered.

The Canadians had covered nine miles in two days. But now "Operation Totalize" was stalled. Simonds' "set piece" had broken down in the absolute irrationality of war.

It took Simonds a week to organize another joint infantry-tank-air force operation to open the way to Falaise. Once again, armoured carriers successfully moved the troops forward. And once again, Allied planes bombed their own men. The yellow "recognition" smoke that identified Canadian troops was almost identical in colour to the yellow "target indicator" smoke used by the air force. No one had thought to colour-code the campaign. Of the 811 planes that attacked, 77 British aircraft, including 44 from the Canadian No. 6 Bomber Group, bombed the Canadians by mistake. This time, misdirected bombs killed even more Allied soldiers than American planes had killed a few days before in this highly planned, strategic military campaign.

Despite the interruption, by August 16, Radley-Walters, Bartlett, Dextraze and the other Canadian soldiers were on the outskirts of Falaise. Two months before, the 12th SS had had 20,000 men and 150 tanks in Normandy. Now, the remaining 300 to 500 men and a dozen or so tanks were caught in Falaise, squeezed between the Americans advancing from the south and the British and Canadians from the north. For two nights the British bombarded Falaise to block the German escape. Then Dextraze and his company of Fusiliers, supported by Radley-Walters' tanks, moved into the rubble to capture or kill the last German soldiers.

Dextraze had about 60 men. Seven had been with him since he landed in France; the rest were fresh recruits. In six weeks he had lost 113 of the men he had so diligently trained.

"We had bugger-all as far as troops," recalls Dextraze. "Normally, if you've got enough men you just surround a building and make sure the Germans are not going to get the hell out of there. To take it — well, I don't like it very much. I hadn't done any street fighting, no house-to-house fighting."

Holed up in a girls' convent school near the centre of the city, 50 *Hitlerjugend* covered their comrades' retreat. The school was surrounded by a thick stone wall and commanded the main road through Falaise.

"It's only one building, made out of stone. You've got to move in there. You're a 24-year-old guy, you are the best damn infantryman that the world has ever known, and you've got the best men with you. You can do any damn thing. But within five or ten minutes — you get two men wounded, two killed ..."

Dextraze felt the weight of his men's lives in his hands. More than anything, he admired military leaders with daring and conviction, resourceful men who did much with little.

"I had to figure out how the hell to go from one bloody room to another. You try to go slowly, you've got to be patient. There's techniques, we learned that in England, but we never practised them. I'd open the door, throw a grenade. You take

In the five day battle to close the Falaise Gap, Canadian soldiers took 14,000 German prisoners.

your chances but you've got to go one by one. Finally, five, six hours, I cleared the thing."

Four *Hitlerjugend* escaped; they had drawn lots to see who would break out to tell Meyer of their fate. The rest fought until they were killed. None surrendered.

One memory haunts Dextraze from Falaise — the main square, lit brightly by bomb fires, a statue of William the Conqueror presiding over the smouldering ruins. On one side stood a large church, its steeple toppled. Inside were frightened, wounded civilians.

From their position in the town hall, the Germans opened fire, "really pouring it down on us, and we at them," remembers Dextraze.

Then, all of a sudden, "fire stops coming from them and we stop our fire, too. Nobody's firing."

Dextraze looked up to see why the guns were silent.

"A kid had come out of the church, right into the square. About four, five years old, its little finger in its mouth, standing right between us, just looking left and looking right.

"And all of a sudden a woman came out. The mother, I suppose. Grabbed the child, put it to her chest. Looked to the left. Looked to the right. And ran back into the church."

The mother and child were gone. The church door closed.

"Then, the Second World War resumed — the Germans on one side and us on the other, trying to kill each other. Seeing the act of that mother, you think how stupid all the shooting was ...

"The Germans did not resist very long. Full darkness came. And that was the end of it."

THE TASTE OF VICTORY

The Canadians took Falaise, helping to block the main German escape route eastward to Paris. The castle where William the Conqueror had been born, on the high rock or *falaise*, was shot to bits; the city below, in ruins.

On August 17, 1944, Allied air crew counted 2,200 German vehicles retreating in broad daylight through the narrow gap of the Dives River Valley, south of Falaise — "like rush hour on a bank holiday." A hundred thousand German soldiers were desperately trying to escape through the Falaise Gap. "The Allies bombed it. They shelled it. They did everything," says Bartlett.

Battle lines changed hourly. In the confusion, Allies repeatedly bombed their own troops — 77 Canadians died from mistargeted bombs; 209 were wounded.

By early August 19, Canadian and American soldiers were only two miles apart on either side of the narrow river valley. By evening the Gap was closed. The way out, a slaughterhouse.

"Civilians. Cattle," remembers Bartlett. "Put it this way. You could walk through it, but you couldn't drive through it without driving over bodies."

Hundreds of green-uniformed corpses carpeted the ground. And in the approximately 30 square miles of the Gap, British Operational Research investigators counted 187 tanks, 157 lightly armoured vehicles, 1,778 trucks, 669 cars — a total of 3,043 guns and vehicles. No count of the dead or wounded. In the next five days, the Canadians alone took 14,000 German prisoners. In all, 50,000 surrendered.

The Battle of Normandy, often called the "Stalingrad of the Western Front," was as apocalyptic as Passchendaele and Vimy Ridge. Between June 6 and August 25, when Paris was liberated, 200,000 Germans were killed or wounded, another 200,000 taken prisoner. A week after liberation, the Allies estimated that 206,703 of their men were wounded or killed.

"Unlike the British or the Americans, we were continuously engaged," said Simonds, "so we took a higher proportion of dead and wounded. Our divisions in Normandy suffered 18,444 casualties; 5,021 were killed."

This was victory.

General Jacques Dextraze served the rest of his working life in the military. He retired as Chief of the Canadian Defence Staff in 1979. The son he fathered on his honeymoon, and saw for the first time three years later, joined the United States Marine Corps and volunteered to fight in Vietnam. He was killed in action.

For Dextraze, the war years remain the happiest of his life.

To his way of thinking, "the German soldier was doing his job. He was a mercenary, the same as I was. It's that simple to me. There will always be wars; always have been."

Dextraze was awarded a Distinguished Service Order for his attack on the church in St. Martin.

"It's not very popular to say it now, but most of us believed in God. That's what helped us get through the bad parts. You've got to believe that this whole thing didn't happen by chance. That there's order in the thing."

Brigadeführer Kurt Meyer was convicted of war crimes and served nine years in Dorchester penitentiary in New

Members of The Highland Light Infantry celebrate victory with a toast of Calvados.

General Radley-Walters survived
the war and was decorated with the
Military Cross by General Bernard
Montgomery.

Brunswick. During that time, his advice on warfare was discreetly sought by Canada's Department of Defence. He was released in 1955. While celebrating his 51st birthday, Meyer suffered a fatal heart attack. He was given a hero's funeral by his SS comrades.

After the war, General Radley-Walters became Colonel Commandant of the Royal Canadian Armoured Corps and then retired to a farm near Killaloe, Ontario. Recently, he returned to the war graves of Normandy. What struck him were "rows of men under 25 — mostly teenagers." He says the war brought "a terrible lot of grief and blood and tears and hate among the people. But we mustn't forget the heroism, the sacrifice and the courage of the soldiers of both sides. And now, 46 years later, that comradeship has moved to our former enemies and we stand as friends together."

Bruce Ducat, a survivor of the Black Watch attack on Verrières ridge, can hardly talk about it.

"At night I don't sleep because I have a hard time with the ... This is the only time I've talked about it. And when I went to the cemetery at Bretteville, in Normandy, oh geez, I cried buckets. There was nearly all my platoon in there."

Viril Bartlett, survivor of the Novies' attack on Tilly, has six sons, none in the military. He doesn't dwell on the war.

"My children don't even know anything about it."

After the war, Donald Pearce completed a doctorate in English literature, then moved to California to teach at UCLA. During the Battle of Normandy, despite army regulations forbidding journals, he maintained his sanity by writing. From his "arthritic trench," he reflected on the common assumptions about war — that war is necessary, that it reduces life to its essentials. And, mired as he was in the unrelenting obsession of how to destroy potential destroyers, he knew all such theories were "perverted." He wondered if he would hear them again in the course of his lifetime.

"If I do, I will certainly recognize them at once. They originate with people who are driven by something inside to embrace destruction lovingly, who are craving death, the sight of it, others' deaths, their own; with those who worship savagery because they are sick of reason."

When Pearce's journal was published in 1965, he dedicated it to

his 19-year-old son, who was then confronting the possibility of going to his own war.

"A job has been done on Europe, on the world, and the resulting trauma will be generations long in its effects. It is not just the shock of widespread destruction, of whole cities destroyed, nor the shock which the defeated and the homeless must have suffered, that I am thinking of: it is even more the conqueror's trauma, the habit of violence, the explosion of values, the distortion of relations, the ascending significance of the purely material, the sense of power, and the pride of strength. These things will afflict the victors as profoundly and for quite as long a time as the other things will afflict the victims; and of the two I am not sure that a crass superiority complex is the more desirable.

"Perhaps I underestimate our ability to return to normal again."

When Germany finally surrendered in May, 1945, Europe was left littered with the debris of war. For many Canadians, the scars they brought home with them would never heal.

Epilogue

No history is free of bias. The military historian whose "facts" may be indisputable omits the lived experience of the foot soldier. The social historian who writes about everyday life is accused by the specialist of painting with too broad a brush. The oral historian who evokes actual experience through direct quotes, in fact selects and shapes. Reality, ultimately, rests on point of view.

In *The Valour and the Horror*, Brian McKenna tells his truth about Canadians in the Second World War — the untrained teenagers sent to Hong Kong, an inevitable massacre; the air crew of Bomber Command, lied to about their mission; the foot soldiers of Normandy, battling Germans in the brutal irrationality of conventional war.

"The country must know war in its fullness," says McKenna. "Let us celebrate the valour. But let us speak the evil and the horror. People will be torn by these two things. But let them know what war is really about. Because without knowing, we'll fall into it again."

McKenna feels a responsibility to the soldiers who shared with him their private agonies.

"I hold them in such reverence," he says. "These ordinary guys from Buctouche, and British Columbia, from Pointe St. Charles and Cape Breton, from Ontario and the Prairies, being thrown into total war, bearing the unbearable, carrying the horror around inside them all these years."

In *The Valour and the Horror*, McKenna exposes the propaganda images and technological seduction of war.

"As we worked on the films, the Gulf War erupted. So much was reminiscent of the Second World War, the strategies, the censorship, the images created. What most people remember from the 1991 Gulf War is the 'smart' bomb. Yet only 7 percent of the bombs were 'smart' or accurate. The other 93 percent were conventional iron bombs — and three out of every four missed their military targets. They killed civilians. Women and children — blew them to smithereens.

"The Dambuster raid was the 'smart' bomb of the Second World War — low-flying, bounced off the water, neat, did its job. The book about the Dambusters sold 5 million copies. The movie broke all attendance records. It convinced people that most of the bombing in the Second World War was geared to knocking out industrial targets, when the policy as early as 1943 was really to kill as many women and children as possible, to bomb Germany to its knees.

"Yet, the Dambusters and the 'smart' bombs are the images of war people carry around in their heads."

The Valour and the Horror counters war propaganda and rhetoric. McKenna hopes his work will uncover the true Canadian memory of war. He traced his own family's war past through Adrian, whose grave he finally located in Belgium, planted with red roses and marked with a white stone tablet engraved with a single maple leaf. Thousands of Canadian soldiers are buried in Belgium, Holland and Northern France, their graves maintained by the Commonwealth War Graves Commission. But in their own country, there is little to remind Canadians of their experience of war.

"Where can Canadians touch the past? In the First World War, we were only 9 million people and we lost 66,000 soldiers, more than the Americans in Vietnam. The Americans have a Vietnam War Memorial, a wall with 58,000 names on it. Every day, even now after 15 years, people go up with tears in their eyes and touch the names, evoking the past.

"I want my daughters and my son to have in their bones the story of their country and what it's gone through. They are all equal before the possibility of going to war and getting slaughtered. I want their generation to be equipped to ask questions, to understand in an emotional and intellectual way what it means to go to war. If they're ever faced with that, they'll have to make their own decisions. What I can do for them is pass on the information, the feeling, the horror of what these guys suffered.

"I had to tell this story. The pain and grief suffered by those who went to war and all their families form part of our subconscious as a nation. I had to say, 'Here's what we went through. Never forget it. And if we're ever tempted to do it again, remember what the cost is.' "

McKenna knows that passing on the lessons of war is not an easy task. Once it starts, the buildup toward war is like a storm. And when the fighting is over, it is impossible to describe what it was really like.

"War is so horrid, so awful, that it staggers your wildest imagination. All the films that have been done, all the books written, can't even come close to conveying the horror of war, because we organize the insanity until we've turned it into a story that seems to have a beginning, a middle and an end. And in the end it doesn't. It's just this thrashing, bloody insanity.

"God help us if we forget that. God help us."

Photo Credits

The publisher has made every reasonable attempt to locate copyright holders. Any information on missing sources would be much appreciated.

PROLOGUE:
p. 4 courtesy of R. Del Tredici

CHAPTER ONE:
p. 7 courtesy of Mary (Gray) Magnusson; p. 8 courtesy of Yvonne Hogle; p. 9 (top) PA116790, (bottom) courtesy of R. Manchester; p. 10 courtesy of R. Clayton; p. 11 courtesy of F. Reich; p. 13 PA C49740; p. 16 PA C49742; pp. 17-18 all courtesy of D. Languedoc; p. 22 Japanese Army Film; pp. 25-26 courtesy of D. Languedoc; p. 27 PA114878; p. 28 courtesy of W. Jenkins; p. 29 PA114877; p. 30 courtesy of Mrs. A.B. Scott; p. 31 PA116795; p. 36 Japanese Army Film; p. 37 (top) PA145352, (bottom) D. Languedoc; p. 38 courtesy of Kay Christie; p. 39 courtesy of L.V. MacKay; p. 40 courtesy of D. Languedoc; p. 41 PA116796; pp. 42-45 all courtesy of D. Languedoc; pp. 46-47 all courtesy of Yvonne Hogle ; p. 49 courtesy of J. Stroud; p. 50 courtesy of F. Reich; p. 51 courtesy of Betty Standish; p. 53 PA137745; p. 54 PA151738; p. 55 courtesy of D. Languedoc; pp. 57-58 courtesy of R. Manchester.

CHAPTER TWO:
p. 65 (top) courtesy of D. Harvey, (bottom) PL27614; p. 66 (top) courtesy of J. Moffat, (bottom) M. Favreau PL28114; p. 68 (top) IWM CH18685, (bottom) PL22511; p. 69 courtesy of K. Brown; p. 70 CWHM; p. 72 PL29954; p. 74 (top) PL26262, (bottom) PL26273; p. 75 PL42445; p. 77 PL42146; p. 78 courtesy of F. Dyson; p. 80 PL42038; p. 81 IWN C4552; p. 83 PL29938; p. 84 courtesy of F. Phripp; p. 85 (top) PL43185, (bottom) PL29662; p. 86 CWHM; p. 87 PL43952; p. 89 PL42402; p. 90 PL42839; p. 94 PI33463; p. 98 IWM MH7294; p. 99 PL28114; pp. 100-101 all courtesy of Ken Brown; p. 104 (top) IWM CL2500, (bottom) IWM CL3400; p. 109 PL42407; p. 110 PL43186; p. 111 PL1144275; p. 116 source unknown.

CHAPTER THREE:
p. 122 (top) courtesy of S. Griffin, (bottom) courtesy of B. Ducat; p. 123 courtesy of J. Dextraze; p. 124 PA132786; p. 125 PA132456; p. 126 courtesy of V. Bartlett; p. 127 courtesy of S. Radley-Walters; p. 128 PA133757; p. 129 (top) PA132654, (bottom) J. LeBouthillier; p. 130 IWMB 5111; p. 131 (top) PA116533, (bottom) IWM B5251; p. 132 PA133954; p. 133 IWM B5386; p. 134 PA169293; p. 135 PA140855; p. 136 WA1068 CWM; p. 140 PA132727; p. 141 courtesy of D. Pearce; p. 142 PA132912; p. 143 (top) PA136042, (bottom) B5425; p. 144 PA131537; p. 146 PA140870; p. 147 PA131397; p. 150 (top) PA132906, (bottom) PA132731; p. 152 PA116543; p. 153 PA141665; p. 155 PA141712; p. 158 PA129130; p. 161 PA131398; p. 163 PA114495; p. 165 PA138272; p. 166 PA128092; p. 167 CAOP52715N Concordia University.

KEY: P.A./Public Archives of Canada; P.L./Canadian Forces Photo Unit; C.W.H.M./Canadian Warplane Heritage Museum; I.W.M./Imperial War Museum; C.A.O.P./Canadian Army Overseas Photo Unit

The Valour and the Horror

A TELEVISION SERIES DIRECTED BY BRIAN MCKENNA

Produced by: Arnie Gelbart and André Lamy

NFB Producer: Adam Symansky

Written by:

HONG KONG: Brian McKenna and Terence McKenna

BOMBER COMMAND: Brian McKenna and Terence McKenna

NORMANDY: Brian McKenna, Terence McKenna
and Roman Jarymowycz

Cinematography: Neville Ottey

Sound: Ian Challies and Robert Jones

Art Direction: Robert Hackborn

Costumes: Michael Harris

CBC Manager: Nancy Dinunzio

CBC Supervisor: Darce Fardy

Produced by Galafilm Inc.
Co-produced by
Canadian Broadcasting Corporation
and
National Film Board of Canada
in association with
La Société Radio-Canada
and the participation of
Telefilm Canada